S0-BTZ-531

*Nine Steps
to Effective EDP
Loss Control*

Tom S. Eason

Douglas A. Webb

Nine Steps to Effective EDP Loss Control

digital

DIGITAL PRESS

Dedication

As "moonlighting" authors who had to spend time aside from our regular jobs to write this book—hours that we would otherwise have spent with our families—we dedicate this book to Gladys, Anne, Beth, Lindy, Brian, and Karen who gave up some of their rights to our time so that we could "do our thing."

Copyright © 1982 by Digital Equipment Corporation

All rights reserved. Reproduction of this book, in part or in whole, is prohibited. For information write Digital Press, Digital Equipment Corporation, Crosby Drive, Bedford, Massachusetts 01730.

Printed in the United States of America

10   9   8   7   6   5   4   3   2

Documentation number EY-00006-DP

The manuscript of this book was created on a Digital word processing system and by means of generic coding and a translation program was automatically typeset on Digital's DECset Integrated Publishing System.

Library of Congress Cataloging in Publication Data

Eason, Tom S.
  Nine steps to effective EDP loss control.

  Bibliography: p.
  Includes index.
  1. Electronic data processing departments–Security measures. I. Webb, Douglas A. II. Title. III. Title: Nine steps to effective E.D.P. loss control.
HF5548.2.E224 1982   658.4'78   82-18330
ISBN 0-932376-25-8

Preface

Sociologists and commentators on the current scene labeled the 1970s the "me" decade, concisely summarizing the focus of many people on achieving personal satisfactions. For the manager, however, the 1970s were hardly the "me" decade, but a tough and demanding time full of challenges and pitfalls. Pressures of all kinds appeared, grew, and showed no promise of easing in the near future. Government regulation of business rose to new highs, partly in response to public mistrust and partly as a manifestation of the juggernaut character of big government. Some slackening is now under way, but the level of regulation remains very high. The growth in activity to establish and monitor professional standards has added to these pressures.

Closely related is the increasing emphasis on oversight—by boards of directors, audit committees, stockholders, and public interest groups. These groups are applying pressures to make more profits, control costs, expand business, and serve the public interest. The pressures of competition demand that market share be maintained or expanded, new products and services be offered, and new market areas, even new countries and cultures, be opened up to expand business opportunities. The public sector exerts similar pressures, primarily to get more value for each tax dollar. Moreover, great strides forward in technology, especially in the information processing field, have given the manager a variety of options, but a variety of headaches, too. Proliferation of computers in the work environment may solve many problems, but it also creates many others. Inflation and the increased cost of energy have forced closer attention to tight management of resources. Finally, in most cases, the manager is dealing with a changing consumer public. The growing number of two-income families is generating more disposable income and thus increasing the demand for product quality and for "luxury" goods and services.

All these pressures lead to new rules, new roles, and new responsibilities in almost all areas of management. This book deals with one important area, that of electronic data processing (EDP), and focuses on security, control, and audit of EDP systems. We have adopted the term *loss control* for the management process that covers all three aspects. The goal of loss control is the systematic, comprehensive, and economic control of noncommercial losses. By *loss* we mean the compromise of an asset through destruction, use, or modification by authorized persons or unauthorized persons in unplanned or unauthorized ways; through denial of use to authorized persons; through disclosure to unauthorized persons; or through simple theft.

Our objective is to start the manager thinking and *acting* about EDP loss control as a means of:

1. Retaining profits already earned
2. Ensuring that profits yet to be earned will be secured
3. Protecting organization assets from "bad luck" and from incompetent, undermotivated, and dishonest people
4. Strengthening the manager's stewardship of the organization's assets
5. Adding to the level of control of the EDP environment, thus making the lives of managers (both within and without EDP) easier.

We have identified nine fundamental steps leading to effective EDP loss control. These steps came from much experience in working with organizations to analyze and help solve their problems. The primary basis of this experience has been management consulting and research conducted when we were part of the Information Systems Management Department of SRI International (formerly Stanford Research Institute). The nine steps evolved from a series of one-day boardroom briefings to chief executive officers, board members, and senior managers of more than sixty major U.S., Australian, and Canadian corporations.

The nine steps provide the organizational framework of the book. The introduction presents a conceptual model of the loss control process and some essential definitions. Chapters 1 through 9 discuss the steps in sequence and describe the techniques appropriate for application. These steps reflect three major phases: foundation and framework (chapters 1 and 2), organization and implementation (chapters 3 through 8), and review (chapter 9). A final chapter summarizes, offers some general advice, and considers cost-benefit issues.

This book can be of value to any manager who uses EDP to control assets, to provide management information, or to conduct operations. The greater the involvement of EDP in the organization, the greater the exposure to loss, and the greater the value of conscientious use of these principles. Yet our experience has shown that most managers do not realize the extent of their EDP-related exposures and have not taken sufficient measures to reduce them. Maximum value will result from *applying* the approaches discussed here directly to your problems and opportunities as a manager. Use this book as a spur to your thinking. As you read, ask yourself, "How can I apply this to my situation?" Chapters 1 through 9 conclude with outlines of analyses that you can perform to assess the EDP loss control posture of your organization. Followed through, these analyses will help you start taking the right steps to reduce exposures.

We gratefully acknowledge the contributions of several others to this book. The staff of Digital Press offered much consultation and many good editorial suggestions. Several reviewers, chief among them LeRoy Rodgers of Digital Equipment Corporation, Terry Colvin of Synergy, Inc., and Dean Robinson of TransAmerica Corporation, made valuable contributions to its form, style, and content. We value their suggestions but accept full responsibility for the final product.

Tom S. Eason
Atherton, California

Douglas A. Webb
Livermore, California

Contents

Figures

Introduction

Structure and Definitions

Before we discuss the nine steps promised in the title, a description of the structure of the book will provide some insight into its order and logic. Figure 1 shows the structure and basic elements of a program to control EDP-related losses: a foundation, a framework, components extended from the framework, and a review element. The foundation of effective EDP loss control is appropriate attitudes. This first step is covered in chapter 1. Chapter 2 discusses the framework itself. Six basic components extend from the framework and give it substance: risk management, allocation of responsibilities, development of control standards, constructive interaction, effective EDP audit, and priority attention to systems development. These components are covered in chapters 3 through 8, respectively. Chapter 9 presents the final part, the review element, which entails periodic evaluation and updating of loss control activities. The concluding chapter deals with implementation, costs, and future trends.

Because this field is comparatively new, there is much variation in terminology. Our working definition of *loss control program* is: a formalized business structure and process designed to help an organization manage, limit, and control losses. Chapter 2 expands this definition in a full discussion

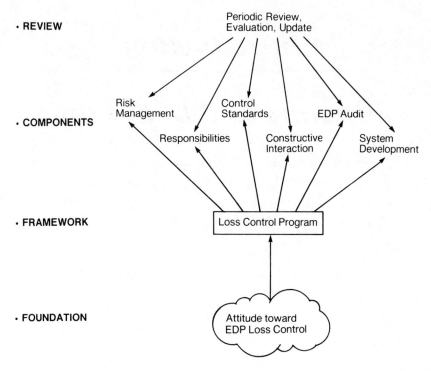

Figure 1. *Structure and basic elements of an EDP loss control program*

of the topic. Other terms used in this book are defined below. We urge you to spend more than just a few moments reviewing these definitions. Are there any surprises?

Asset: Anything of value, including people, programs, documentation, control mechanisms, data processing capability, and intangible items such as the good name of the organization.

Confidentiality: The status of data in terms of secrecy and privacy provided. (This is a technical issue, unlike the sociopolitical issue of privacy rights.)

Control: A mechanism to protect assets through deterrence, prevention, or detection of threat events and to limit losses through swift recovery. The purpose is the reduction of exposure. Controls can be implemented through hardware, software, policies, and procedures.

Detection: One possible purpose of a control; discovering and recording or otherwise making known a security compromise.

Deterrence: One possible purpose of a control; producing a state of mind that discourages the performance of an act that could compromise security.

Exposure: The financial effect of a cause or threat event times the probable frequency of its occurrence. The value need not be quantitative.

Hazard: A source of risk.

Integrity: The status of resources and assets as complete, unbroken, accurate, and error-free and of people as properly trained, trustworthy, and functioning correctly.

Loss: A compromise of an asset through destruction, use, or modification by unauthorized persons; denial of use to authorized persons; disclosure to unauthorized persons; or simple theft.

Prevention: One possible purpose of a control; stopping or forestalling an event that could compromise security.

Privacy: The right of individuals to decide what information about themselves they wish to share with others and what information they are willing to accept from others. (This is not a technical issue, in contrast with the issue of confidentiality.)

Recovery: One possible purpose of a control; regaining or replacing a resource, asset, or capability after a security loss.

Risk: The chance or probability that a loss will occur.

Security: The status of resources and assets as safe and protected by proper control.

Threat: A potential source of loss of assets.

Threat event: The act of a source (either a person or a natural force) that exploits a vulnerability in the system of controls that protects assets; a loss may result.

Vulnerability: A weak or missing control that could be exploited or otherwise result in a loss.

A Perspective on Chapter 1

This executive realizes that Pinkley cannot be counted on to further the organization's goals unless the right attitude is established. If the topic of the meeting is EDP loss control, then the executive is addressing the proper first step—shaping the right corporate attitude. (From "Frank and Ernest" by Bob Thaves. Reprinted by permission. Copyright © 1981 NEA, Inc.)

1

Establish the Right Corporate Attitude

It is a fact of life that illegal and immoral acts in the business world are more and more frequent and are often overlooked, condoned, or even secretly envied if the target is a business (especially "big business") or a government agency. At the same time a gradual decline in worker involvement, productivity, craftsmanship, and job loyalty has added to the likelihood of errors and omissions in business activities. It is in this context that interested people must view the processes, disciplines, costs, and benefits of EDP loss control. The importance of EDP loss control can be summed up in three *m*'s— money, motivation, and morality.

An effective program of EDP loss control can pay dividends (quite literally) in the form of expenses not incurred, omissions and errors not suffered, and frauds and defalcations not perpetrated. No one has ever made a convincing estimate of the total cost to business of the intentional and unintentional loss-causing acts associated with EDP processes, but it is clear that the cost is high. The losses from errors and omissions are probably significantly greater, but they are intrinsically unmeasurable. In any case, the stakes are large; the money message is there for all to read.

Motivation is a bit of a buzzword these days, but it stands for a most important business concept, namely, that people work more productively when they believe in what they are doing and in the people for whom they are working. An intelligent, well-planned, and well-presented program of EDP loss control is evidence that the management of the enterprise is inter-

5

ested in the efficient functioning of business processes, that it has certain reasonable expectations of the participants in those processes, and that the long-term success of both the enterprises and the participants is linked through cooperative efforts such as control of EDP-related losses.

Morality is a difficult subject to deal with, but to say that it is old-fashioned and out of place in a book directed toward business managers is unjust both to today's managers and to the businesses they direct. The great majority of businessmen today realize the importance of ethical business principles and practices. A program of loss control, properly oriented to constructive goals and away from punitive ones, can serve as a statement from the enterprise that it intends to maintain high standards in dealing with its communities of customers, suppliers, and employees. Many important companies have taken great pains to make their principles clear. IBM, for example, states its corporate credo thus: "Dignity and respect for the individual. Pursuit of excellence. Dedication to service."

To provide a firm starting point, this chapter examines where EDP loss control fits in the overall business process; discusses corporate goals, objectives, and strategies as the bases for a program of loss control; and explores the "right" corporate attitude by examining principles that should shape that attitude. We offer a model for the loss control process both to provide a context for the corporate attitude and to underscore management's role as the initiator and the loop-closer in the process.

Where EDP Loss Control Fits in the
Overall Business Process

The strategic business process is built on a flow of ideas and action that begins with goals, moves toward objectives, formulates strategies, defines programs, and then executes the programs. (See the accompanying "Model for the Business Process" for background on these concepts.) An examination of the character of EDP loss control activities shows that EDP loss control fits most naturally in the scheme of things as a program, that is, as a group of coordinated activities aimed at carrying out strategies of reducing or avoiding costs and risks. Of course, for such a program to exist at all implies that it must have one or more goals, objectives, and strategies to justify its existence and to drive it to the execution, evaluation, and looping stages. Subsequent chapters describe the content of the program itself, but success depends to a large degree on the establishment and implementation of goals, objectives, and strategies.

Many organizations have adopted formal planning processes in which serious consideration is given to the statement of corporate goals and objectives. If your organization is one of these, you are well structured for the EDP loss control process. If not, build a logical "tree" structure, proceeding

A Model for the Business Process

One effective way to characterize the business process is to use a mnemonic, GOSPEL, which serves as an acronym for the six basic steps in the process. These steps are:

Goals
Objectives
Strategies
Programs
Execution and evaluation
Looping

Webster's defines *goal* as "the end to which a design tends; aim; purpose." In the context of corporate strategic planning the term acquires a more precise meaning: goals involve broad policy statements by the organization. IBM's corporate credo, cited above, is a goal statement. Goals must pass a simple test. Ask, "Why are we doing this?" If the answer is "Just because," then it is a goal. If there is a more explicit answer such as "To increase profits by 10 percent" then it is not a goal but an objective. Objectives are more specific. They almost always include some criterion for success that establishes a more or less quantitative measurement of the degree to which the objective is achieved. The rules of strategic planning require that objectives proceed logically from goals. Usually several objectives are associated with each goal.

A strategy is a way to achieve an objective. Strategies are always associated with specific objectives. One objective may have one or more strategies tied to it. An objective without at least one strategy is unachievable. Profits can be increased (an objective) by lowering costs or raising prices (strategies). Costs can be lowered by taking advantage of economies of scale through manufacturing larger lot sizes, by introducing economic order quantity disciplines, by implementing more effective inventory controls, or by controlling EDP-related losses (programs). Programs are specific courses of action that the organization can take to implement strategies. As with objectives in relation to strategies, each strategy should produce one or more programs.

Execution and evaluation are the "doing" parts of the process. Execution is simply carrying out the program, and again there is a correspondence between programs in the prior step and execution activities in this one. In turn, evaluation of each execution activity entails asking, "How did we really do against our objectives? Did we really implement all of our planned programs to the fullest extent?" The final step is looping—feeding back the results of evaluation in order to profit from mistakes by doing better next time or to profit still more by reapplying current successful actions. This step may involve adjusting programs, inventing new strategies, or even modifying objectives.

from one or more goals through the corresponding objectives and strategies leading to the program. Use this reasoned structure as one means to form and encourage the right corporate attitude toward EDP loss control. This examination of goals and objectives can be done best with broad support from top and middle management, but it should be done regardless. In the last analysis, the program of EDP loss control must be "sold" to all managers, since its existence depends on the support and funds allocated to it by top management and its success hinges on the cooperation and support it receives from all members of management.

Money, motivation, and morality are the stimuli. The structure of goals and objectives supported by the loss control program provides the context. Establishing the appropriate corporate attitude is the first step.

What Is the Right Corporate Attitude?

Successful EDP loss control programs are founded on four principles that contribute to the right corporate attitude.

1. Loss control must be widely understood to be an important part of the business.
2. Loss control is everybody's job.
3. Loss control is more effective when it is based on a constructive rather than punitive approach.
4. Loss control is most effective and efficient when attention is given to deterrence and prevention as well as to detection and recovery.

The first principle seems so obvious that it ought not to have to be stated. However, a comprehensive study conducted by SRI International for the Institute of Internal Auditors in 1976 disclosed that, although almost all companies gave lip service to the principle, only 17 percent of the respondents to the survey of large users of EDP had any kind of a loss reporting system that would reliably, exhaustively, and frequently assess the level of EDP-related losses in their company. The absence in an organization of an effective loss reporting system is a strong indication that management does not consider control of losses to be an important part of the business. Of course, management can also affirm the importance of EDP loss control in many other ways, including promulgation of organization policy on loss control and active support for policy enforcement. Chapter 2 deals with these matters.

The second principle reflects the fact that no effective program of loss control can succeed if it assumes that the responsibility for success lies with some small cadre of "loss controllers" such as EDP auditors and computer security officers. There is a strong analogy between the processes of successful loss control and those of quality assurance. The United States is learning much today (a lot of it from our Japanese competitors) about enhancing quality and productivity by involving large numbers of people at the working level. As long as clerks, programmers, computer operators, and other non-managerial personnel feel that losses are being absorbed by the company and will not particularly affect them either now or in the future, the most vigorous and well-planned loss control program will fail.

The third principle embodies the idea that the purpose of a loss control program is to control losses, not to catch someone doing something wrong. Behavior modification, rather than elimination of the people who make the errors, is the most useful approach in implementing the program. The elements of the loss control program must be constructive: "Will this action enhance understanding of, and respect for, the needs and procedures of our business and thus promote better conformance to our standards of performance?" This is not to say that penalties for serious and deliberate violations should not exist and be well understood by all parties; without a penalty structure, no system can be made safe from a small amoral minority. But corporate and individual attention should focus on the positive and constructive aspect of the process. Loss control is a problem that involves people; as such, it needs solutions that will also involve people and take into account how they think and behave. Furthermore, experience shows that problems can often be approached as opportunities in disguise. The third principle emphasizes this aspect.

Closely allied to this principle is the fourth, which states that the loss control program should give proper attention to deterrence and prevention as well as to the more traditional avenues of detection and recovery. Deterrence and prevention are related strategies. Deterrence deals with influencing the state of mind of a potential perpetrator or person about to make a mistake; prevention deals with taking overt measures to put obstacles in the way of a potential perpetrator. Emphasizing deterrence and prevention has at least two advantages. First, it conforms to the principle of constructiveness and

---

An Example of the Four Principles at Work

A combination of agencies within a European bank—the physical security group, the management information systems (MIS) director, and the head of internal audit—first independently and then jointly alerted top management to an increase in EDP-related losses. Management responded constructively by calling in a loss control consultant to make an independent evaluation. The evaluation agreed in most respects with the joint appraisal. With encouragement from the board of directors, management used the in-house groups and the consultant to develop a broad program intended to build awareness and involvement as a prerequisite to further specific actions. The emphasis was to be on deterrence and prevention, implemented through educational efforts, published policies, and the strengthening of physical and logical access controls.

---

thus allows all parties to deal with one another in an atmosphere of trust and mutual respect. Management may say, in effect, "We all realize that in the course of our daily duties we may be exposed to situations where our actions or inactions could cost the company substantial amounts of money. This loss control program is designed to provide support for all employees in taking the right actions." Second, deterring or preventing an inappropriate act is almost always less expensive than detecting and recovering it afterward.

The more familiar detection controls are often employed in a context of entrapment. Recent noteworthy examples of this approach include various police-conducted "stings" and the Abscam scandals. EDP systems lend themselves rather well to the inclusion of traps for people who deliberately attempt to defeat the controls of a system. The construction of such traps in systems usually requires large amounts of time and money. It is worthwhile to consider whether those same resources could provide better results if they were applied to deterrence and prevention. In any event, if entrapment is to play a significant part in the program, the fact that traps are present should be made common knowledge throughout the organization. Alerting employees to the situation will have a maximum deterrent effect and offer at least a minimal concession to the principle of constructiveness.

The Context for the Right Corporate Attitude

Developing and maintaining the right corporate attitude requires the involvement of corporate management in the loss control process. Figure 2 shows a conceptual model of this process.

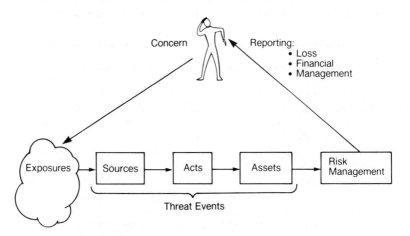

Figure 2. *Model of the loss control process*

The most obvious characteristic of the model is its circularity. As a continuing process, it is subject to continual correction. Starting at the point where management manifests concern with losses, the model proceeds through a series of logical steps. The first step recognizes a variety of exposures. These exposures are realized by threat events. A threat event has three components: source, act, and asset. A source performs an act to threaten an asset. This sequence of possible events drives the process of risk management, leading to reports to management that, in turn, close the loop of the model. Thus, management has two roles in the loss control process, that of initiator and that of loop-closer. To fulfill its proper role in the loss control process, top management must demonstrate continuing concern about losses and a readiness to provide direction and priorities and must assess results in loss, financial, and management reports.

Figure 3 shows the model at a more detailed level. The categories listed are exhaustive to ensure their usefulness as guidelines in the formulation of a complete loss control program. The nine categories of exposures, taken from W. C. Mair, D. R. Wood, and K. W. Davis, *Computer Controls and Audit*, 2d ed. (Altamonte Springs, Fla.: Institute of Internal Auditors, 1976), are broad concerns whose emphasis will vary considerably from organization to organization. Sources must be either acts of nature or of people. If people are involved, their skills, knowledge, and access to assets are the critical factors that determine the character of the act.

Acts are either intentional or unintentional. A programmer may build a control weakness into a program either deliberately for later exploitation or through inadvertence, laziness, or carelessness. An effective loss control program deals with both contingencies and involves two fundamentally different control measures, because the types of acts are fundamentally different.

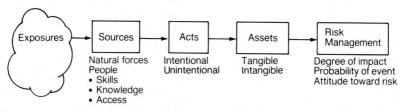

Exposures
- Erroneous record keeping
- Unacceptable accounting
- Business interruption
- Erroneous management decisions
- Fraud and embezzlement
- Statutory sanctions
- Excessive costs/deficient revenues
- Losses or destruction of assets
- Competitive disadvantage

Figure 3. *Loss control model details*

The Loss Control Model at Work
in an Organization

One of the nation's ten largest life insurers has, over the last three years, built an excellent EDP loss control program based on appropriate corporate attitudes. The architect of the program, a senior financial officer, used his long experience with the firm to carry out an educational campaign that created broad support among top management. He fostered a system of loss reporting and related reports to involve managers at several levels in dealing with the problems, and used reported losses (in the company, in other insurance companies, and in the literature) to focus attention on specific exposures of special importance to the company. This led to support for increased funding for EDP audit activities, EDP operations security improvements, and studies of exposures in key applications systems. His success depended in large part on building proper attitudes among managers and involving them in loss control activities as initiators and loop closers.

Intentional acts are less frequent, generally involve larger amounts of money, and involve people working at the top of their skill level. Unintentional acts, on the other hand, are more frequent, usually involve smaller amounts of money, and involve people working at their lowest levels of skill. Controls effective with unintentional acts may have little impact on intentional ones, but controls effective with intentional acts are often at least partially effective against unintentional acts. This fact justifies additional attention to protective measures for intentional acts.

Assets can be tangible or intangible. Tangible assets are easy to identify—dollars, goods, and data. Data constitute a tangible asset because collection, processing, and storing almost always cost money. If data are lost or destroyed, re-creation also involves cost. Intangible assets may be just as valuable but are harder to assess; these include customer goodwill, the list of customers itself (very valuable to a competitor), and opportunities (to invest, to secure greater market share). Risk management (the subject of chapter 3) involves determining the impact of losses and the probability of loss events, and quantifying (to the extent possible) the corporate attitude toward risk.

Establishing the right corporate attitude to EDP loss control is founded on the bases discussed above. First, management must understand the place of EDP loss control in the overall business process. Second, basic principles should shape the corporate attitude. Finally, management should provide the proper context for action in loss control.

In contrast to the two brief success stories presented above, the following case study describes an organization with a poor attitude toward loss control.

CASE STUDY

Background

☐ A large multidivision retailer that had grown substantially by acquisition in the last ten years had many styles of management and several semi-independent data processing installations throughout the United States and Canada. Headquarters was trying to unify and standardize operations in all the divisions by performing processing in a single center and reducing the outlying data processing locations to input/output stations. The company had no formal sustained loss control activity and little knowledge of the rudiments of EDP security. The board of directors approved funds for the program development, and the vice-president of management information systems engaged a consulting firm to help design an EDP security program.

Method

The consultant planned a series of interviews with top and middle management and with nonmanagerial employees both at headquarters and at the divisions. When the time came to schedule the interviews, the client company showed considerable reluctance; it set up a steering committee for the project that demanded advance detailed scenarios for the interviews and recommended permissible topics for the interviews. After much negotiation, the interviews proceeded.

At the same time, review of EDP security practices in the headquarters data processing center turned up many opportunities for improvement in physical and data security in both operations and systems development. Recommendations were grudgingly received and were acted upon slowly and incompletely.

The consultant also began work with the internal audit organization, studying the accounting controls in a few typical EDP systems in daily use and looking at ways in which internal audit could actively contribute to the integrity of controls in systems under development. As the consultant built up a good working relationship with the internal auditors, the real reason for retaining the consultant began to surface: the audit committee of the board of directors, concerned about the implications of the Foreign Corrupt Practices Act for the company's EDP systems, had strongly "suggested" that an outside consultant be called in. Management had turned this suggestion into a project to plan an EDP security program.

Results

The consultant's problems in doing an effective job for this company resulted directly from the lack of a proper corporate attitude toward loss control. There was no question about the Board's attitude; believing that loss control was an important part of the business, it tried to communicate to management that loss control was part of their job. Somehow the message got lost or distorted. Concern about the probable resistance of politically sensitive and independent-minded division executives took precedence over implementing necessary measures to control EDP losses. At the same time, the headquarters data processing center was concerned about maintaining prestige in relation to the divisional operations that it was taking over. Thus, headquarters tolerated bad practices rather than admit that there was room for improvement. There also seemed to be a prevailing belief that the program planning project was punitive, a belief that management could not or would not dispel.

Once the consultant developed an understanding of these impediments, he was able gradually to overcome them. Headquarters EDP people accompanied the consultant on field visits; all interviews were kept completely confidential; and conclusions and recommendations concerning the program were phrased in nonthreatening terms. Finally the steering committee was persuaded to relax its concerns about the project and any possible unfavorable findings and to focus on the potential benefits from a straightforward, constructive approach.

Conclusions

The right corporate attitude toward EDP loss control is a prerequisite to any lasting and positive change in an organization. If that attitude is missing, weak, or not universal among management, education and the fine arts of interpersonal persuasion must be brought to bear to lay the foundation for success. □

Is Your Organization Prepared
for an EDP Loss Control Program?

1. Does your organization have an explicitly stated set of corporate goals? If so, obtain it; if not, try to summarize on paper what you think they are, based on the behavior of the organization.

2. Is there an explicitly stated set of objectives for the current or coming years? If so, obtain it; if not, try to devise one from your knowledge of the organization and from existing documents such as the budget for the coming year.

3. Are strategies specified or obviously in use that imply control of EDP losses? If not, derive at least the broad outlines of such strategies; in any case, commit the outline of those strategies to paper.

4. Identify the major focuses for a program of EDP loss control in your company.

5. Who are the major stakeholders who would be affected by such a program? What are their current attitudes? Compare those attitudes with the four principles. What has to be done to change those attitudes to improve chances of success?

6. Identify managers who are now acting in the roles specified in the loss control process model. Do they catalyze any of the steps in the model? How can they help build the right corporate attitude toward EDP loss control?

A Perspective on Chapter 2

Noah could have been confronted with this situation only if he had had no program. (From "Frank and Ernest," by Bob Thaves. Reprinted by permission. Copyright © 1980 NEA, Inc.)

2

Establish a Loss Control Program

This chapter addresses the basic questions of what a loss control program is and why an organization should have one. It defines the key operational principles of the program and presents the steps for developing it. Establishing the loss control program entails defining organizational functions that will provide and administer control and also offer a supportive context for that control.

A Loss Control Program Defined

A loss control program is a formalized business structure and process designed to help an organization manage, limit, and control losses. The goal of such a program should be the *systematic*, *comprehensive*, and *economic* control of noncommercial losses.

An understanding of these terms is crucial to the nature and content of an effective program. Noncommercial losses are not explicit balance-sheet losses but are extra, avoidable expenses such as those due to errors, omissions, unauthorized acts, and natural disasters. Examples are destruction of a data file, theft of a mailing list, abnormal termination of a program run, or loss of business due to unfavorable publicity regarding the EDP operations of the enterprise. In contrast, commercial losses are directly related to the products and business processes of the enterprise. These include monetary loss due to foreign currency fluctuations, poor pension fund investments, buying rather than leasing a subsequently obsolete asset, or other unprofitable decisions. Business tools, experience, and experts exist to help rectify or prevent commercial losses, but resources are not so generally available to help with noncommercial ones. Yet there is need for an organized approach to the latter kind of loss.

Intuition and experience both indicate that a systematic approach to problem solving is more likely to get results. To be systematic, a loss control program must be consistent and organized. That is, the program must be based on a well-defined organizational structure that can make sound security and control decisions and employ a set of uniformly applied standards and procedures of operation and evaluation. Too often EDP control decisions are made on a hit-or-miss basis. A sensationalized news article appears in the morning press describing an EDP-related loss, x (for example, a disgruntled employee breaks into the computer room and damages computer equipment) that could have been prevented (the writer says) by a control, y (such as another guard on duty, a closed-circuit TV camera, or a stronger door). By afternoon a number of companies have requested quotations for a y type of control—not because they have carefully thought about the occurrence of an x type of loss or because they do not have a y control, but because they are not thinking systematically and do not have an effective organizational structure in place to address their control objectives and needs.

Comprehensive control of EDP-related losses is complementary to systematic control. Comprehensive control deals with all potential losses above a reasonable dollar threshold and addresses these losses wherever they might occur in the organization. Failure to be comprehensive often occurs in application programs (ones that solve business-related problems such as preparing the payroll or managing inventory). Program designers often make the actual computer processing the focal point of control and ignore the fact that the manual phases of originating transactions and delivering output have the most exposure. This greater exposure is the natural consequence of involving people instead of machines in the conduct of a process. Comprehensive control of EDP-related losses results when applications programs are considered in their broadest scope, including all the associated manual processes—such as filling out transaction forms, reviewing batch records, checking control totals, and distributing reports—that must precede and follow the actual computer processing.

Good business judgment dictates that controls must be cost effective: they must cost less than the expected loss they are designed to prevent. Directing as much attention as possible to quantitative methods for selecting controls will help ensure that the costs of control are justifiable in the light of potential losses. Although it is possible to spend either too little or too much on loss control, experience indicates that organizations more often spend too little. Chapter 3 lays the groundwork for dealing with this problem.

What's in a Name?

Loss control is the more suitable term, but it is wise to remain flexible. In a consulting assignment to produce a set of loss control policies for a large bank, the consultant learned one day that all references to "loss control" had been changed in the documents to "security." The consultant eventually learned that top management would not accept "loss" as a legitimate term: the bank was in the business of profits, not losses! The same kind of logic was probably used when the U.S. government changed the name of the Department of War to the Department of Defense.

Terminology

We use the term *loss control* rather than *security* because it is more meaningful for today's businessperson. *Loss control* is broader in scope, does not carry so many emotional overtones, and does not confine situations mainly to fraud and theft. Businesspeople must focus on appropriate controls for all potential EDP-related losses, whether they result from intentional acts, unintentional acts, or the forces of nature. Losses resulting from natural disasters and from errors or omissions in the EDP facility can be at least as threatening to the success of the enterprise as losses from criminal acts. Working solely from the base of sensational news stories concerning "computer crime" is certain to distort and perhaps cripple efforts at rational control of losses. In the same way, focusing on the "hard" EDP resources (computers, communications, and facilities) overlooks the need to have appropriate controls over application systems (such as financial and materials management programs) and the processes that feed them and distribute their output. Application of the quantitative methods of risk management helps avoid these potential errors.

Program Attributes

The most important attributes of a successful loss control program are:

- A top-down approach
- Formalization
- Organizational support
- Feedback/followup

Top management bears ultimate responsibility for any losses and thus must initiate the program. Success depends on acceptance by all members of the organization. The best way to ensure that acceptance is to initiate and support the program from the top with a formal statement of policy and obvious interest. This principle holds for the duration of the program. For example, developing an EDP disaster recovery plan requires input from many business functions (such as users, EDP, and insurance). Those implementing successful programs have found that a short but direct memo from the chief executive officer, authorizing the project and directing all staff to cooperate fully, goes a long way in ensuring the project's success.

Formalizing the program requires making policies and documenting standards and procedures. Formalization not only emphasizes the intent to have a strong program; most important, it gives clear direction to the staff responsible for implementing and executing it. ■ A durable goods manufacturer lost most of the impetus of a well-launched loss control program because insufficient resources were allocated to formalization; as a result, policies and standards were a long time reaching the people who were to be charged with their application.

Support for the program entails an unequivocal organizational commitment of time, energy, and ideas by management and staff, and of money and facilities. Management should think carefully about making such a commitment of resources and should not proceed unless willing to stand by the decisions in both good times and bad. A halfhearted or fair-weather effort can be counterproductive. This is an especially important consideration during difficult economic times. It often seems that time and money spent on loss prevention and detection are somehow wasted, and they are therefore a likely target when budget cuts are mandated. At such a time, reexamination of the effectiveness of the program is certainly in order, but the underlying logic of the need for the program cannot be open to question.

Basic management principles prescribe that results be measured and factored into subsequent actions. Feedback implies setting up monitoring and evaluation mechanisms that provide timely, accurate reports. The internal audit department, EDP quality assurance, and regular business reports (such as loss reports) are the sources of this feedback. As with any business system, feedback is essential to measure how well the elements are functioning and to provide a sound basis for modifications. Follow-up is the other side of the equation; modifications have to be implemented and a follow-up mechanism helps ensure that the loop is really closed.

Why Have a Loss Control Program?

There are two essential reasons for having a loss control program:

1. A loss control program produces beneficial results.
2. A loss control program satisfies the concerns of stakeholders in the organization that management is doing its job properly.

The first is a purely positive reason; the second is motivated by pressure. In today's demanding business environment, it is often pressure rather than a simple positive motive that catches attention and provokes action. Nevertheless, the positive reason deserves first attention. Organizations that have implemented EDP loss control programs have learned that it is reasonable to expect several beneficial results in exchange for the costs of setting up and administering a loss control program. These include:

Better knowledge about loss: What losses are occurring, where and when they occur, who is associated with their occurrence, and how they occur are facts essential to planning and executing preventive and corrective steps. ■ A major supermarket company found, after instituting a loss reporting system, that lack of sufficiently effective controls over inputs to an automated purchasing system was resulting in significant losses; there was excess inventory in some commodities and out-of-stock conditions in others. When purchasing agents were given more training in the use of the system and data base integrity was improved through tighter procedures, stocking levels were improved with a lower inventory investment.

Better attitudes about loss control: Middle managers and staff will become more alert and concerned about the problem and good things will happen. Business programs in quality control, safety, and other areas have demonstrated that this is the case. Loss control can be looked at as a people problem or a people opportunity. In either case, everything possible should be done to promote a positive attitude in the people concerned. ■ By analogy with the practice of forming quality control "circles," a computer manufacturer involved systems analysts, programmers, and EDP operations people in regular dialogue about reducing EDP-related losses. As a result, several important improvements in control integrity in key applications were identified and brought into effect.

Less risk: The program will help managers identify areas where they can reduce risks prudently. ■ As a result of installing a loss control program in its plant, one manufacturer identified an unnecessary risk associated with its purchasing procedures and eliminated it at no cost through a procedural change.

Less uncertainty about risk: The program will provide identification of risk areas so that the risks being accepted are better known and some descriptive information regarding them becomes available for better decision-making. ■ A large Japanese bank was experiencing a high incidence of teller-initiated transaction correction. Management assumed that this was due to teller errors, although the possibility existed that someone was using the system to defraud the bank. After intensive analysis of the character, frequency, and nature of the transactions, management felt confident that they were not being used to cover fraudulent activities. The analysis also brought about redirection of training efforts and an overall throughput improvement for the teller staff. Fewer erroneous transactions also resulted in less overtime for tellers in the end-of-day balancing process in the bank branches.

Less vulnerability: The program will uncover vulnerabilities and suggest ways to reduce them. ■ As a result of examining programs that processed certain special communications charges, a common carrier was found and eliminated a logical error that occasionally permitted underbilling.

Lower losses: Although only subsequent experience will suggest how much has been gained, the prudent executive must agree that better knowledge, better attitudes, less risk, less vulnerability, and less uncertainty have historically added up to lower losses. It is reasonable to expect a lower level of loss and organizations should demand that a loss control program produce such a result.

Several problems preclude an outright statement that an EDP loss control program is cost-beneficial. First, most companies do not even know what their losses are; the study cited in chapter 1 found that only 17 percent of a sample of large EDP users had a loss reporting system. Second, probability rather than certainty is involved in many instances. As a result, cost-benefit conclusions must be based on averages, expectations, and the like, rather than on hard fact. The biggest difficulty arises when the average event is tolerable but a very unlikely nonaverage event occurs. Remember the man who drowned in a lake whose average depth was only three inches! There are many such events whose disastrous consequences must be protected against at almost any cost, among them loss of the company receivables file or the loss of integrity of manufacturing control in a very large business. Finally, it is nearly impossible to assign a value to good stewardship of company assets. If a person pays his or her auto insurance premiums faithfully and never has an accident, was it cost beneficial to take out insurance in the first place? If management prepares a sound EDP disaster recovery plan and the company never experiences a disaster, was it cost beneficial to produce the plan?

The second and often triggering reason for implementing a loss control program is the concerns of the stakeholders. Their interests may make the cost-benefit question a moot one. The stakeholders may be the management of a holding company, stockholders, directors, employees, customers, the government, or a public-interest group. They may be motivated by enlightened self-interest, the force of law or government regulation, concern for personal liability, or an animus against big business. In any case, the pressure to bring losses under control is real and requires a response.

Key Operational Principles of a Loss Control Program

Analysis of many individual loss control efforts indicates that the success of an EDP loss control program depends on the employment of eight basic principles in its structure and operation. Each is discussed in more detail in later chapters. They are:

1. Risk management is fundamental to effective loss control. To the extent feasible, deliberate, careful, complete tabulation of assets, threats, vulnerabilities, and controls provides the data base, and the principles of decision analysis provide the tools to make informed decisions about risk.

2. A clear mandate fosters understanding and support for loss control. A statement of purpose and support from top management provides direction and impetus.

3. Orderly, logical allocation of responsibilities for loss control lays the groundwork for success. When everyone knows what is expected of him or her, results come more easily, promptly, and smoothly.

4. A set of well-chosen standards and guidelines gives direction and thrust to a loss control program. Common rules and procedures help people to do their jobs.

5. EDP, users, auditors, and risk managers must communicate frequently and effectively. Loss control is a multidisciplinary process that demands interaction and contributions from many people.

6. Competence of program participants is essential. Good people should be selected and trained, and outside resources made available for their professional betterment.

7. A portion of program resources should be allocated to the audit and control of EDP systems development. Loss control needs better systems to work with; this is the only way to get them.

8. Program performance should be evaluated regularly. Unless success is measured against some agreed-on standard and the results fed back into program direction, money and time are likely to go to waste.

Principles for Effective Loss Control

1. Apply risk management disciplines.
2. Define a clear mandate.
3. Allocate responsibilities.
4. Develop standards and guidelines.
5. Organize for good communication.
6. Promote competence.
7. Give attention to systems development.
8. Evaluate regularly.

Steps in Developing an EDP Loss Control Program

Principles neatly reduce complicated issues to simple statements. Starting a loss control program is not so simple. It is a process involving people, organizations, and motivations. Experience from many implementations indicates that the following sequence is a good one for most organizations.

There are seven steps. The first is to secure the commitment of top management. Chapter 1 described how to work toward that commitment by establishing the proper attitude. Without commitment nothing much can happen; with it, the leadership of the organization supports the program. That commitment must be an informed one; what the program will cost must be clear, as well as what it may save. The commitment should be written and public—preferably an endorsement of the program and its organization, or promulgation of a general loss control policy.

The creation of a general loss control policy should be the second step in the program. Excerpts from one policy appear in the case study presented in the next section. Senior management should initiate and direct the policy's formulation.

The third step, development of a loss control policy specifically aimed at EDP and related functions, follows as a natural outgrowth of the general policy. The policy should be developed by staff from EDP, computer security, insurance, EDP audit, and the organization's general security function. The loss control policy for EDP should begin to deal with specifics but must remain a policy-level document, giving guidance and setting forth management's expectations for performance. The case study below also presents an example of this type of policy.

In much the way that treatment of an illness begins with taking a medical history of the patient, control of losses begins with identifying and characterizing losses. For this, a loss reporting system is necessary, and creating this system is step 4. The reporting system may take various forms, but many successful systems have certain properties in common. It must use a broad definition of assets subject to loss. In particular, in addition to money, it must include in the definition of assets such nonmonetary items as customer lists, computer programs, and other important business records. These kinds of data have intrinsic value and generally are expensive and time-consuming to replace if lost, or will result in competitive disadvantage if compromised. ■ In the early 1970s a medium-sized services business in southern California lost its accounts-receivable file through a processing mischance and had no backup copy. The company was forced to ask its customers how much they owed and to accept the amounts reported as correct. The loss was never accurately estimated, but the company nearly went bankrupt.

The loss reporting system should be made formal and automatic—ad hoc systems tend to work when they are most needed—and should incorpo-

Asset	Application System (if appropriate)	Date	Source: • natural disaster • job title	Act: • modify • destroy • disclose • take • deny usage • use	Intentional Unintentional	Responsible Department or Area	Area of Vulnerability	Amount or Value Lost	Corrective Action Taken or Planned
Money	Purchasing/Receiving	5/14/82	Purchasing Clerk	Take	Intentional	Purchasing	Authorization of entry of new vendor data	$15,000	Strengthen controls on authorization. Check compliance more frequently.
Data	Accounts receivable	5/24/82	Computer operator	Destroy	Unintentional	Computer operations	Lack of proper write protection on transaction summary records	$2,000	Change program to insure that transaction summary records are fully protected.

Reporter J. Hootman

Figure 4. *Sample EDP loss report form*

rate a reasonable threshold, below which data are not reported. Federal banking regulations, for example, require that only losses in excess of $1,000 be reported. Business judgment should be applied to achieve a happy medium between acquiring nonsignificant data and overlooking material losses. Figure 4 shows a form for reporting EDP losses as they occur; filling in the form is the responsibility of line management in the area where the loss occurs. Figure 5 shows a form for analyzing, summarizing, and periodically reporting losses to top management. These forms provide one effective source of feedback to initiate corrective actions.

The loss reporting system should encompass the full scope of EDP. Staff from the computer security department can coordinate preparation efforts, but staff from user departments as well as EDP functions must also be involved.

The fifth step is to allocate responsibilities for loss control. There are many concerned agencies: internal audit, EDP audit, security, legal, insurance, EDP, quality assurance, personnel, and all the agencies that are users of EDP services (such as the accounting and manufacturing departments). The general principles of definition of responsibility apply. It is helpful to consider the allocation of responsibilities from the standpoint of clarity, completeness, consistency, and closure. The responsibilities must be clear and unequivocal—each person in the enterprise must understand what is expected. They must be complete—no gaps, no overlaps. They must be consistent—all parties should be working together toward the same goal. Finally, there must be closure—fulfillment of responsibilities must be monitored and evaluated. These are simple criteria applicable to any organizational structure, but they are often inadequately fulfilled. The criterion of closure—allocating and carrying out responsibility for measurement of success and for corrective feedback—is most often overlooked. ■ In one instance, a consultant, called in to evaluate a continuing loss control program for a large manufacturer, found that no one had been assigned the responsibility of tabulating and analyzing losses and violations, and that consequently, the program was running as an open loop.

Often the clear allocation of responsibilities is difficult and must involve several iterations. For example, defining responsibilities in both user and EDP departments so there are no gaps and no overlaps will take time and several trials. Nonetheless, the task should be an important management objective.

Providing support to the program is step 6. Support is of four kinds: leadership, competence, time, and money. The program needs a full-time head whose salary depends on the program's success. It cannot succeed without competent people; it cannot be a "parking place" for ineffectives. Time, dedicated time, of workers and management must be devoted to its success. The same holds true for financial support.

Period 2Q 1982

Asset	Responsible Department				Area of Vulnerability										Number		Amount	
	Purchasing	Computer operation	Applications programming	Systems programming	Handling of input data	Handling of output	Handling of machine-readable data	Physical access to facilities	Logical access to internal data	Access to application programs	Access to systems programs	Data communications	Business ethics	Backup & recovery	Period	Year to Date	Period	Year to Date
Facilities				1								1			1	1	10,000	10,000
Supplies																—		—
Hardware																1		5,000
Systems programs																—		—
Application programs			1							1					1	1	2,000	2,000
Data		1												1	1	2	2,000	3,000
Money	1				1										1	1	15,000	15,000
Property																—		—
Services	2					2									2	4	7,000	11,000
People																—		—
Intangible																—		—
Other																—		—

Figure 5. *Sample summary EDP loss report form*

Steps in Developing an EDP Loss Control Program

1. Secure the commitment of top management.
2. Develop a general loss control policy.
3. Develop an EDP loss control policy.
4. Create a loss reporting system.
5. Allocate responsibility of loss control.
6. Provide support for the loss control program.
7. Monitor and evaluate progress.

Skeleton Outline for an EDP Loss Control Program

Introduction
  Background
  Purpose
  Scope

Environment
  Shaping management attitudes
  Shaping staff attitudes

Policies
  Developing general loss control policy
  Developing EDP loss control policy

Organization
  Definition of structures
  Definition of responsibilities

Support
  Resources
  Training program
  Communications

Interfaces
  Responsibilities of interfacing organizations
  Services provided to interfacing organizations

Major Activities
  (categorized by responsible organization)

Schedule and Budget
  Major milestones
  Financial plan

Finally, follow-up and feedback are essential once the program is in motion. Step 7 consists of evaluating progress and quality of work, drawing conclusions, and feeding back corrective actions to improve the value of program outputs. This step can be the most useful of all. One of the most effective ways to implement it is through a loss control steering committee, made up of concerned managers meeting regularly to deal with policy matters and to assess the progress and direction of the loss control program. Several organizations find this approach valuable and productive. Success has been greatest when the committee has a clear charter and is composed of people who believe in the mission and act accordingly. A purely nominal steering committee is counterproductive and can significantly set back security and control efforts. ■ One large bank's security committee did not meet for over a year. Managers from several departments reported that they assumed that the committee was functioning well and addressing control issues. They had not been overly concerned, but in reality the bank was taking a number of unnecessary risks.

CASE STUDY

Background

□ One large foreign bank was a confederation of hundreds of cooperatives similar to credit unions, banded together as a central processing and controlling agency to provide nationwide quality service not attainable through individual institutions. Over 3,000 individual bank branches were involved, almost all of them quite small. The client company had multiple regional processing centers and was a substantial user of EDP technology to meet its processing demand. Bank management perceived the existence of potential problems resulting from the organization's heavy dependence on EDP and sought advice from a major consulting organization.

Method

The consultants found that management had a constructive attitude toward control in EDP processes, and that the traditional security function and the EDP function within the bank were prepared to work cooperatively with each other but needed a broader viewpoint and guidance. Some piecemeal security-related changes had been made in EDP facilities and systems, but no comprehensive plan was in effect.

Results

The consultants determined that the necessary focus would best be supplied by a cooperative effort to develop and promulgate general and EDP loss control policies for the bank. The consultants led a team that prepared these policies. The general loss control policy, issued as a formal statement by the bank's senior management, emphasized the overall goals and objectives for the organization. The EDP loss control policy particularized these goals and objectives for the EDP service group and its users. Excerpts from the two policies follow.

General Loss Control Policy

Introduction

The senior management of the Bank, issuing this statement of policy, emphasizes as its ongoing and vital responsibility to the member local banks to preserve and safeguard the assets of this organization . . . .

The senior management of the Bank therefore considers this loss control policy to form an essential part of the overall policy framework of the Bank. We will initiate and/or maintain those measures which provide for the maximum security and utility for the respective categories of Bank assets, consistent with the operational requirements of the organization, and when the components of the policy can be determined to be cost-effective within a reasonable time frame.

Goal

The goal of this loss control policy, therefore, is the control in a systematic, comprehensive, and economic manner of noncommercial losses.

Objectives

The objectives of this loss control policy are to:

1. Identify risks that can permit a loss of Bank assets, and analyze their potential impact on the organization.
2 Minimize the probability of an incident's occurring.
3. Minimize losses should an incident occur.
4. Transfer or share with an outside organization part or all of those risks where the potential impact of a loss to the Bank cannot be reduced to an acceptable level.

Responsibility

General: Each person or organizational entity assigned a responsibility is empowered with the corresponding authority to adequately execute the responsibility.

Every head of an organizational entity is assigned primary responsibility for those aspects of loss control implementation falling within the domain of that entity. One or more entities may also be assigned secondary responsibility for relevant tasks, such as for reviewing operations or advising and coordinating on related issues.

Senior responsibility: The Board of Directors have overall responsibility for loss control within the Bank.

Line responsibility: The head of each directorate or comparable organizational group has the primary responsibility for developing, implementing, and executing a loss control policy within the directorate in accordance with the framework of this policy and their respective functions, and for the establishment of corresponding standards and procedures mandated by the policy.

Tasks to be accomplished in the performance of these responsibilities are to be addressed in the annual policy documents produced by the directorates for planning purposes.

Functional responsibility: Specific directorates, staff groups, and departments—Legal, Audit, Personnel, Labor Affairs, and Security—have functional loss control responsibilities.

The head of each functional entity is charged with advising the board of directors upon request regarding the entity's implementation of this loss control policy and specific responsibilities listed below. . . .

Auditing department. Specific responsibilities of the Auditing Department of the Bank emphasized by the policy include:

1. Reviewing, testing, analyzing, and evaluating controls within the organization that are designed to protect against loss.
2. Verifying compliance of Bank organizations with applicable laws, rules, and regulations and with the intent of this policy.
3. Recommending, where applicable, the strengthening of controls and control procedures . . . .

Security department. As established within the Bank, the Security Department is totally oriented to issues of loss control. The head of the Security Department is, within existing hierarchical lines and in accordance with oral directions, responsible to the president of the board of directors for:

1. Providing advice and guidance to management regarding issues of loss control.
2. Maintaining a general awareness of the potential for losses and advising line and staff organizations where specific risks are identified.
3. Consultation regarding the execution of this loss control policy.
4. Investigation of variations from this loss control policy and associated standards and procedures.
5. Coordinating, advising, and providing crisis management in cases of major incidents, such as large fires, strikes and kidnappings.
6. Assisting internal and external groups in the investigation of fraud and other intentional acts causing losses to the Bank, without prejudice to the task of the Auditing Department.

7. Administering the physical security function for Bank facilities and for senior management personnel.
8. Maintaining contact with various outside organizations that can provide assistance to the Bank regarding loss control matters.
9. Interacting with the Insurance Department regarding the type and amount of insurance appropriate for loss control.

EDP Loss Control Policy

Introduction

...Assets are defined in a broad way and include personnel, cash, securities, computer programs, data on magnetic tape, disks, punched cards, or in transit, computer facilities, supplies, data communication equipment, documentation, computer time, and intangible factors such as the public reputation of the Bank.

Goal

The goal of this loss control policy is to economically reduce to an acceptable level potential losses that might impact the provision of data processing services.

Scope

Data protection: The integrity and confidentiality of all data in all forms in centralized systems, from transaction acceptance or message acceptance at remote sites, through processing and storage, to dispatch of output or receipt of message at remote sites.

Technical development: All phases of the system development life cycle from problem definition through post-implementation evaluation for all automated systems.

Objectives

Security: Insure the security of the personnel, facilities, supplies, and equipment comprising the EDP Department.

Control of development and maintenance: Insure that for hardware, software, firmware, and operations procedures:

1. The process of maintenance and development is done in a controlled way.
2. The products resulting from maintenance and development have the required levels of control.

Issues

The basic aspects of loss control are integrity, security, confidentiality, and continuity. Integrity refers to the quality or state of resources or assets, for example, data, software, systems, etc., as being complete, unbroken, and error free, and to people as being properly trained and functioning correctly.

General

Cost Effectiveness

1. Evaluate all risks and associated controls from a cost-effectiveness point of view. This impacts both the quality and quantity of controls and resources to be used.
2. Insure that sufficient but not excessive controls and resources are applied. This, however, must not compromise the personal safety of Bank staff or customers. . . .

Data Confidentiality

1. Identify different levels of secrecy classification for Bank and customer data. This entails defining the corresponding levels of secrecy to be maintained.
2. Categorize each type of Bank and customer data into one of the levels of classification and provide the corresponding level of secrecy.
3. Insure that information is distributed to Bank personnel and to outside personnel only with the approval of the appropriate line managers responsible for the information. . . .

Conclusions

Development of these policies provided a point from which the diverse groups within the bank could begin active cooperation on matters of loss control. Understanding of positions and responsibilities was improved. The bank as a whole also developed a stronger concentration on matters related to loss control. After the policies were promulgated, the succeeding steps in the loss control process went smoothly for the most part, and the bank today has an effective, functioning program. □

A Checklist

As you evaluate the posture of your organization toward EDP loss control, use the following questions, grouped by topic, to sharpen the focus of the evaluation and to contribute to its completeness. These questions should be used to provoke thought and to raise issues for consideration. This is not a checklist in the sense that you can set aside each item after having dealt with it once.

Policies

1. Does your company have a loss control program?
2. Is it explicit or implicit, systematic or haphazard?
3. Is it based on policy, and if so, how widely circulated and understood is that policy?

Objectives

4. If not already clearly stated, state the objectives of a loss control program in your company.
5. Test these objectives against the criterion that control must be systematic, comprehensive, and economic.
6. Why is EDP loss control particularly important in your company?

Definitions

7. Is the broad sense of loss control as opposed to security understood in your company?
8. Are the concepts of loss and asset clearly defined?

Program Structure

9. Write down the broad outlines of a loss control program for your company. Then ask yourself if it meets the following criteria.
10. Does it have a top-down approach?
11. Does it provide appropriate formalization?
12. Does it allow for sufficient support and does it identify the sources of that support?
13. Does it provide for feedback?

Results

14. What beneficial results are to be expected?
15. What concerns of stakeholders will be met through a loss control program?
16. Who are the stakeholders?

Losses

17. What is the quality of your current knowledge about loss in your company?
18. Do you have a loss reporting system?
19. What is the quality of your current knowledge about risk?
20. Have you attempted to quantify any risks?
21. What is your rough estimate of the amount of EDP-related losses?
22. Are there any data to support that estimate?

Risk Analysis

23. How widespread are the knowledge and application of risk analysis techniques in your company?
24. Are there substantial intangible assets requiring protection in your company?

Organization and Support

25. Are responsibilities for loss control activities allocated clearly in your company?
26. Are funds and skills available, or can they be made available?

Need

27. Do you believe that losses are under control?
28. What data support your conclusion?
29. What trends do you see in the future for EDP-related losses?

A Perspective on Chapter 3

This is an innovative approach, but it just doesn't square with the facts. (From "Frank and Ernest," by Bob Thaves. Reprinted by permission. Copyright © 1978 NEA, Inc.)

3

Understand and Support the Risk Management Process

Before useful action can be taken, one has to be acquainted with the facts. In loss control, the facts come from the careful, analytical treatment of risks associated with EDP systems. Then, loss control measures have to be based on those facts. A basic ingredient in organizing and implementing loss control is the risk management process. It is the manager's responsibility to understand and support the risk management process as a basic part of an effective loss control program. The term *risk management* is sometimes used to describe the use of insurance as a means to reduce the impact of certain types of losses, such as fire, theft, errors and omissions, and the like. We use the term in its broader sense to include all the activities related to identifying, assessing, avoiding, limiting, and offsetting the impact of non-commercial risks on the organization. This chapter examines the risk management process, especially its importance and composition.

EDP risk management may be formal and well reasoned, purely ad hoc, or lacking in any deliberate management of risk at all—risk management by ignorance. The last approach, a form of default analysis of risk, often results when managers give low priority to control and security and make decisions and allocate resources with no apparent conscious thought to control questions. The manager is making the default decision that the risks are very small—small enough at least that additional controls are not needed, or that there is no need to examine the current level of resources dedicated to control.

Evaluating and making decisions are two important things for which managers get paid and the conscious performance of these functions has an important place in analyzing the EDP environment. Data processing plays a significant part in many businesses, both in terms of a hardware/software/ personnel and in terms of business operations. Its ultimate importance depends on the organization and is one of the first questions addressed in the risk management process.

Donn Parker of SRI International, by analogy with the familiar term *mean-time-to-failure*, has offered the graphic term *mean-time-to-belly-up* as a measure of an organization's susceptibility to EDP loss. How long could your organization stay in business if its data processing capability were not available? However extreme such a question may be, it helps make the point that the EDP function is critical to your organization. To meet this concern, some constructive form of risk management is necessary.

Purpose and Benefits

EDP risk management is always done, whether the manager realizes it or not, whether resources are spent on that management or not. There are a number of real benefits from performing EDP risk management well:

Better decisions: Systematically analyzing the EDP environment in terms of security and control will result in better decisions regarding risk-taking and control implementation. Better decisions can be measured in terms of cost effectiveness (cost of controls versus level of risk reduction produced by the controls) and the degree to which the achieved level of control accurately represents the desired level of risk.

■ A large New York bank systematically analyzed the costs and risks of losing its midtown Manhattan data processing center and arrived at the sound decision to establish a second site and use each as a recovery site for the other.

Consistency: Using risk management in a continuing mode will produce greater consistency in the decision-making process. Consistency results from allocating resources to controls such that the level of different risks (or potential losses) affecting the assets and resources in the EDP environment is essentially the same. Consistency will improve both over time and throughout the EDP environment. Lack of consistency is generally a major problem in choosing controls, especially when decision makers change and when they depend on intuition to guide their analysis.

■ Lack of consistency is found in an organization that has an expensive magnet detector at the entrance to its computer center but fails to control other access-related threats by running an "open shop" for programmers and conducting frequent loosely controlled tours of the center.

Increased management control: Applying sound risk management principles will result in better management control of the EDP environment—that is, decisions are made and things happen in an organized, rational way. Control for operations, data, hardware, people, and the development of systems is handled prudently and in accordance with the level of risk that management is willing to accept. ■ In a large thrift association many control decisions were being made in a relatively unorganized way. Managers were making association-wide decisions regarding controls based only on their local concerns. To correct these problems, senior management had a comprehensive EDP risk review performed and used the findings as the basis of ongoing control decisions.

Decision review mechanism: Formalizing risk management provides a way to review criteria for risk and control decisions. The more important risk-related decisions need to be reviewed by a number of different people—the decision maker himself, the decision maker's management, senior management, board members, audit committee members, internal auditors, external auditors, regulators, and lawyers. Being able to explain, discuss, and justify why risk decisions were made is very important to the purpose of these reviews. Being able to arrive at these decisions with some analytic tools and formal bases will save time and give the reviewer satisfaction and confidence.

■ In a large European bank, management operated in a very structured manner. The EDP department was having difficulty obtaining approval for its loss control activities until it started using a formalized risk assessment approach that generated support data that could easily be reviewed by senior management.

Decision documentation: Formalizing the analysis provides documentation for risk and control decisions. Auditors, regulators, and stockholders are making more and more requests for justification of such decisions. Trying to document decisions some time after the fact is difficult. Documentation of the reasons and factors occurs most naturally during the risk management process. ■ The Foreign Corrupt Practices Act (see chapter 5) has led many organizations to adopt more formalized risk management to provide documentation for their security and control measures.

Completeness: Formalizing risk management builds into the control process a means of ensuring completeness. It provides a structured approach to considering all the assets, threats, controls, and vulnerabilities. No process can ensure that every matter will be addressed and, as we discuss later in the chapter, an attempt to do so can be counterproductive. In most cases, however, providing this structure makes it possible to be more scientific and rational. ■ A large Southern financial organization had sound controls over much of its EDP environment but had not focused on the system development area. By using an organized and systematic approach to analyze risks, the company discovered certain high levels of risk and took steps to add appropriate controls in that area, including a formal sign-off policy, EDP audit involvement, and user testing.

Quantification where reasonable and possible: Formalizing the risk analysis part of risk management leads to a more quantitative approach. Ideally, managers would like to have a fully quantitative basis for making risk-related decisions. In some areas of business (such as insurance coverage and securities investments) quantitative approaches are possible and being used regularly. In the EDP area there is less experience with quantitative approaches and the results have not been as useful. However, to the extent possible and for those items that can be meaningfully measured, quantification has proven beneficial. ■ A bank in New York City, during its analysis of fire risks in its EDP facility, found that the city fire department had useful data on the occurrence rate of fires in high-rise office buildings. The bank was able to use these data to analyze its risks.

Continuity: Applying risk management techniques helps ensure that the loss control process is performed continually. The test of any business is its record over time. Too often there is a spurt of EDP security activity (often triggered by news media coverage of a "computer crime" or a computer disaster) followed by a slack period—from benign neglect to outright termination of control expenditures. When risk management techniques become an integral part of the operation of an organization, continuity is fostered. A constant feedback mechanism facilitates and encourages sustained attention. ■ An eastern insurance company has had an excellent record of EDP security and control. The company prides itself on this record and uses risk management to help ensure that it maintains that position.

Model of the Risk Management Process

We define *EDP risk management* as a systematic process of analyzing the EDP environment (assets, threats, risks, vulnerabilities, and controls) to help management in the loss control process. *Risk analysis* we define as a tool to be used in the risk management process to produce a measure of risk or expected loss. The relation of risk management to risk analysis is like that of an engineer to calculus: a risk manager uses risk analysis to solve problems. In this manner risk analysis is seen as the calculus of risk management.

Although there is no uniform agreement on the definitions of risk management and risk analysis, we use these because they allow the broadest and most effective perspective on the process of EDP loss control. The definitions that follow are broad for the same reason.

Assets are all tangible or intangible items of value or use to the organization. These include both monetary and non-monetary items—tapes and disks, company name, data, and goodwill. This broad definition should encourage managers to consider all aspects of their scope of responsibility and to think in terms of responsibility for assets. ■ In translating material on loss control for a foreign bank, we replaced the English word *assets* with the phrase "things of value" because there was no exact one-word equivalent. This translation proved appropriate and helpful in orienting management's thinking to a broader scope and not just to money.

A *threat* is a potential source of loss or reduction in value of assets. In dealing with risk, it is easier to think in terms of individual threat events, as in the model shown earlier in figure 2. In that model a threat event is a source (such as a person) committing an act (either intentionally or unintentionally) that threatens an asset. Typical examples include an operator loading the wrong tape and causing a file to be modified incorrectly; an input clerk dropping a deck of cards; a fire producing extensive smoke and water damage in the building housing the data center; and a programmer modifying a savings deposit program to credit funds to his or her account. Less typical but important examples include business lost because an on-line banking system was down extensively and the hardware vendor could not make necessary repairs; processing interrupted by a work stoppage among key personnel; and business lost and a company name damaged by publicity about a computer related crime.

A threat is always to be thought of as something that could or might happen. It may also be thought of as a concern—the thing that keeps you awake at night, the question you are afraid stockholders will ask about at the next annual meeting, the story about your organization that you do not want to read on the front page of the *New York Times* or *Wall Street Journal.*

A *risk* is the chance or probability that a loss will occur as the result of a threat. Risks, then, involve uncertainty—a very difficult but common problem for management. Risk can be expressed in very precise terms, such as percentages or odds, or qualitatively, in terms such as "high," "medium," and "low."

A *vulnerability* is the weakness or absence of a control that should be protecting assets. Vulnerabilities always exist; there is no such thing as 100 percent security. Identifying and assessing the importance of vulnerabilities involves a negative search—a search for something missing. It is easy to identify the lack of an adequate physical access control (such as a guard) at the entrance to a data center; when logical access controls (such as administrative procedures for the use of passwords) for data are involved, pinpointing a deficiency may be much more difficult.

A *control* is any mechanism, device, procedure, or structure implemented to reduce risk and loss. Again, we make the definition very broad to encourage managers to consider all aspects of their scope of responsibility and to think in terms of responsibility for assets.

Figure 6, the model that describes the risk management process, is a feedback loop with five elements. The two on the left are input elements: assets must be identified and valuations assigned; threat events must be tabulated, their probabilities and impacts estimated. Given these inputs, risk assessment proceeds, by estimating the likelihood that the assets will be subjected to the threat events. This assessment yields the raw material for management decisions about risk. The results of these decisions over time yield risk experience. Experience is also obtained vicariously through other organizations. Loss reports summarize this experience and feed back to improve the estimates of threat event probabilities and impacts and asset identification and valuation. Thus, the model becomes *iterative*. When new information is available or the environment changes, the process should be repeated.

The following subsections discuss each element of the model in more detail.

Inputs

Asset identification and valuation: As a first step in asset identification and valuation, carefully survey the EDP environment to identify EDP resources (such as, computer central processing units, tape drives, disk drives), resources dependent on EDP (such as, the good name of the organization, the capability to process applications, programs), and resources controlled within the EDP environment (such as, data). Second, assign a value to each asset. The standard measure is monetary. Use checklists based on

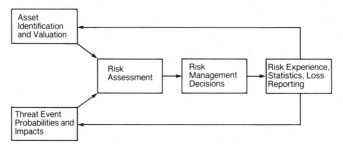

Figure 6.   *Model of the risk management process*

inventories of equipment, files, programs, and other important assets as a starting point. Question the appropriate group of managers (armed with checklists and inventories) to obtain a fairly complete set of assets. Valuation is sometimes more complex. Some items have time-independent dollar values readily available; in some cases, however, values will change over time. For example, losses may vary significantly depending on whether computing power is not available for 1, 8, 24, or 48 hours, or if it is unavailable at a given time such as at year-end closing.

Nontangible items require more thought, and careful analysis. To assess the level of concern for computer crime and its negative publicity, for example, a manager can answer the question, "Would you rather suffer a business loss of $10,000 or be named in a report of a computer crime of $3,000 in the *Wall Street Journal*?" Nontangible assets can often be valued by estimating how much it would could cost to restore the situation to the preloss condition or by estimating the value of the asset to a competitor.

Threat event probabilities and impacts: Obtaining threat event probabilities and impacts means determining some measure of how often a loss event will occur and what effect that event will have on the organization. Good, full data on these contingencies are often hard to obtain. Some probability figures are available from government publications such as those of the National Bureau of Standards and Fire Safety Board, in trade association literature such as the journals of the Association for Computing Machinery and the Bank Administration Institute, and academic studies. Local fire and police departments can also be an important source of hard and recent data. The National Oceanic and Atmospheric Administration has excellent data on the prevalence and destructiveness of severe weather disturbances. When data are unobtainable, intuitive estimates, wide ranges of values (say, "the probability that the event will occur is between 0.25 and 0.60"), or a ranking of different events (such as, "event A will occur twice as often as event B") must suffice.

Quality of data: The accuracy and meaningfulness of both kinds of data can vary widely. In the real world, accurate and quantifiable data often do not exist and cannot be expected to for some time. In such cases one can only try to improve the raw data and use it carefully.

The feedback loop shown in the model is an excellent way of improving the quality of the data. Loss control reports (discussed in chapter 2) can be invaluable. This feedback process must be tailored to the organization and data must be collected promptly.

Another very useful technique is to go to users, who are the "owners" of the applications and assets, to collect or develop the data. The users depend on the accuracy and availability of the data and applications and they are the ones who must live with decisions that are based on the data. It often happens that users do not accept or act upon results of studies done by task forces or security groups. In such cases the users usually comment, "I don't believe the numbers—especially the aggregate figures" or "It just can't be true; you are waving a red flag and it isn't sound from a dollars and cents perspective." And the results may in fact not make sense. The figures may be accurate in an academic sense but inaccurate in a pragmatic one because the users did not participate sufficiently in the formulation of inputs. ∎ In a large retail organization, each division was asked to develop potential loss figures for its operation. The figures were developed in good faith and when reviewed separately appeared sound. However, when taken together they produced results out of line with the overall business volume of the organization. Thus, it is best to go to the users directly for input, data on both assets and threats. They are closest to the information and play an important role in making the final analysis useful. Then, if managers refuse to accept the results of the analysis because the numbers do not make sense, the risk management team can say, "Fine, the numbers are yours, the process is ours and is mathematically sound. Give us some new numbers and we will analyze them." The people collecting data for input should not get emotionally involved. Their task is to get the best data available, refine and check them against past data and industry data, accept the data, and if the numbers must be changed accept that necessity.

Another means of improving the quality of the input data is to use a team approach for research and collection. Using individuals from several functional areas can bring a very positive balance, breadth of experience, and quality control. Functional areas represented on analysis teams can include users, risk management, EDP audit, internal audit, data processing (from systems development to operations), quality control, controllers, computer security, safety, security, and outside consultants.

Risk Assessment

The actual risk assessment is at the heart of the risk management process. It entails combining the input data on assets and threats and producing a measure of risk or expected loss. The result is then used to make risk decisions.

Input data can be combined in several quantitative and qualitative ways. The trend has been from very informal, intuitive qualitative approaches, to highly structured, formal, quantitative ones. We and some other workers in the field believe that trend is now swinging back somewhat, for the reasons discussed below. Qualitative approaches tend to be relatively fast but are prone to error and bias. Assets and threats are often overlooked in the analysis, and the resulting measure cannot be defended or used by others. At the other end of the spectrum is a very attractive conceptual approach—neat, clean, mathematically correct, simple in concept, and promising a quantitative result. The two inputs are represented as:

A = amount (in dollars) of loss resulting from occurrence of a threat event

P = probability (per year) of occurrence of a loss event

The product of the two, $L = P \times A$, equals the expected loss. That is, an organization can expect, on average, to suffer a loss to the asset in question of L dollars in a given year owing to the threat in question. The logical expansion is to calculate the total expected loss (T), the sum of all losses taken over all n assets and all m threats:

$$\sum_{i=1}^{n} \sum_{j=1}^{m} (P_{ij} \times A_i) = \sum_{i=1}^{n} L_i = T$$

This measure (whether for an asset/threat pair or for the total expected loss) can then be used with separately derived information on the cost of controls and on the degree to which they reduce the probability of loss to make security and control decisions. The result is a straightforward cost-benefit tradeoff: if a control costs less than the amount of expected loss reduction, then buy the control; otherwise, look for another control.

Practical problems: In theory this mathematical approach is fairly simple and straightforward; the practice, however, it is not. First, it is not always possible to get the input data in terms of dollars and events per year. Second, dealing with all assets and all threats is usually too big a problem. It is appealing to list every piece of hardware and every data set to get a true picture of the total expected loss, but it just becomes too costly. Moveover, the resulting output is not as accurate as is necessary. The quality of results is directly dependent on the quality of input. Finally, probability data are by nature based on incomplete information, and thus the values are inexact or "soft." Murphy's law notwithstanding, managers do not know for certain that an earthquake will occur and damage a computer center or that an employee will commit a computer crime or that a programmer will incorrectly code a critical part of an application. The final practical problem is a human one. Most people have difficulty basing important security and control decisions on incomplete data and probabilities.

Solutions to practical problems: Even though formal risk assessment has many problems, it can serve a useful function. The following summary guidelines are given in the spirit of our mothers' advice, "Don't go out in the rain . . . but if you do, wear your boots."

1. Don't try to include everything; narrow the scope to a manageable, cost-effective size. Address the major loss control items, perhaps a few at a time in several different efforts.

2. Be sure that users supply the input data. Users are the owners of the data and applications, have the best information, and must live with the results.

3. Use a team to collect and analyze the data. The risk analysis process requires more than just gathering pieces of data and plugging them into an equation. The data must be developed and refined; the more experience and insight brought to this effort, the more useful the data will be.

4. Remember that the analysis process itself is as important as—and maybe more important than—the results. Having a number of different users, EDPers, and managers address loss control systematically and quantifiably is very valuable in developing awareness and pinpointing concerns.

5. Include some sensitivity analysis—that is, consider how critical the input is to the output. If a small change in input values gives a large change in output, you may be on dangerous ground.

6. During the input phase, record why and how values were determined. Such notes are useful for immediate iterations, maintaining consistency, building credibility, and helping the ultimate decision maker interpret output. In addition to raw data, obtain supporting narrative information if possible. Appoint a team secretary to record key factors and reasons leading to the determination of values for asset losses and event probabilities. Put the notes into a usable form and pass them on to the decision makers.

The following discussion and graphs elaborate on items 1 and 5—narrowing the scope and analyzing sensitivity. Figure 7 is a conceptual model and not specific to any one analysis. The figure shows two curves representing two different constant values of expected loss. Each point on a curve is the product of a dollar loss amount and a probability. For example, on curve K,

$$ex_1 = A_1 \times P_1$$

and

$$ex_2 = A_2 \times P_2$$

For any one curve, all the expected losses correspond to all the points on the curve and all are equal. For example, ex_1 equals ex_2, but ex_1 is less than ex_3. There is an infinite number of possible curves, of which K and L are just two, chosen to represent two different situations.

Figure 7 shows the curves K and L dividing the set of expected loss values into three areas, labeled "low," "moderate," and "critical." This means that any pair of loss amount and probability that results in an expected loss less than ex_1 (below curve K) is considered low, any pair that results in an expected loss greater than ex_3 is considered critical, and those in between ex_1

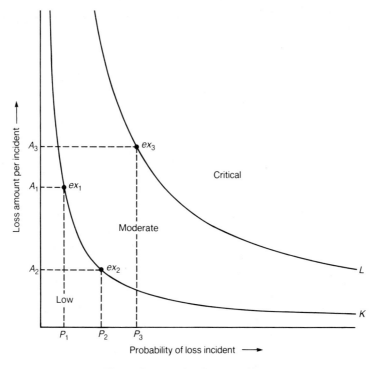

Figure 7. *Levels of expected loss*

and ex_3 are considered moderate. Each organization will have these three areas but the values for the two curves may vary considerably. For example, curve K might represent $1,000 per threat event and curve L, $1,000,000. The choice will be based on the philosophy and risk attitude of the organization—What size of loss it considers low, moderate, and critical.

These curves can now provide some guidance for the risk assessment process. Figure 8 shows the same curves, with the areas now labeled "don't care," "most valuable," and "must control." The values for losses and threat events that result in expected losses below curve K are in the "don't care" area—that is, formal risk assessment is not necessary because the expected loss would be smaller than the cost of the effort to analyze it. At the other extreme, in the "must control" area, the expected loss is so large that controls must be provided, the loss cannot be tolerated, and there is no need to perform a formal risk assessment. The middle section is the most vulnerable area for applying risk assessment. Efforts here should provide valuable information for decision making.

Even in the middle area there is considerable variation in the usefulness of the expected loss data. The upper left and lower right regions of the band represent conditions in which it is most difficult to apply risk analysis and for

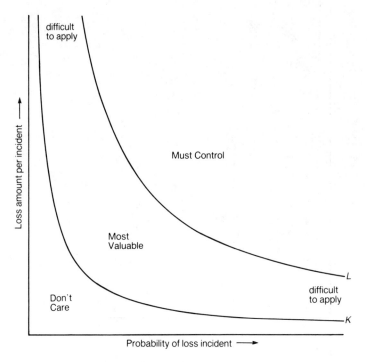

Figure 8. *Relative value of risk assessment*

which the results are likely to be the least useful. In these areas, input data accuracy is low. Dollar values of losses and especially probability values may be the best available, but they are not accurate and are subject to important uncertainties. A small change or more important, a small error in input will result in a disproportionately large change, or error in expected loss. Inaccuracy in input data is inevitable, so formalized risk assessment is precarious.

Figure 9 shows a simplified example. Consider the loss of a major computer center in San Francisco due to an earthquake. (As Californians, we refuse to believe it could happen, but in concession to our geologist friends, we can assume there is a small, but real, probability of its occurring.) It is possible to form a fairly accurate estimate of the loss (A) to the organization, but the probability of the event could easily be P_1, P_2, or P_3 (0.0001, 0.001, or 0.01) depending on the judgment of the expert consulted. Even assuming A is accurate, the expected loss value could be ex_1, ex_2, or ex_3 depending on the probability chosen. This means that expected loss might be in the low, moderate, or critical range. Moreover, no new information is of much value for the decision-making process. Unless there is some assurance that the input data are quite accurate, analysis should be limited to events and assets

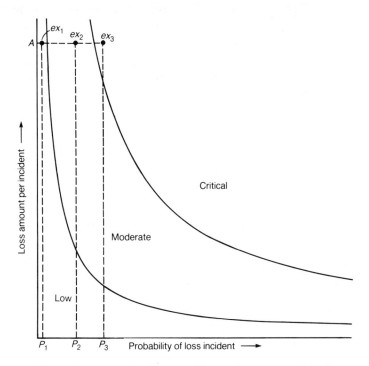

Figure 9.   *Example of expected losses due to an earthquake*

that produce expected losses near the middle of the middle band. Also, it is always wise to consider the sensitivity of the analysis; is there a significant change in the expected loss or more important, would the ultimate decision change if there were a small change in the input values?

Output

The output from risk assessment should be in a form easily usable by decision makers, in terms that can be compared against the costs of controls. The ideal format is dollars on an annualized basis. Because the input data lack accuracy and reflect variation in the probabilities, it is important to include information on the sensitivity of the results. Supporting and intermediate data used to build the final results should also be included.

Feedback

Feedback in the risk assessment process is critical to improving accuracy and usefulness. Few organizations have established formal mechanisms to facilitate feedback. More often, efforts to identify, monitor, and report the information remain uncoordinated, with the result that it seldom gets to the right people. A loss reporting system (discussed in chapter 2) provides an excellent feedback mechanism. Loss types must be well defined and guidelines established for both periodic reporting and reporting exceptional incidents. Feedback should come not only from the normal control functions such as

Applying Risk Assessment in Your Organization

Figure 10 shows examples of items on each axis. Your company's internal audit department can also provide guidance for the two expected loss curves. Have it define a material loss and the level of loss that would make the company fail. The criteria will depend on what your organization's business is and on management's attitude toward risk. ■ One financial institution's policy was: "We don't want to risk having a net loss for the year; thus, the upper limit is the value equal to our profits for the year."

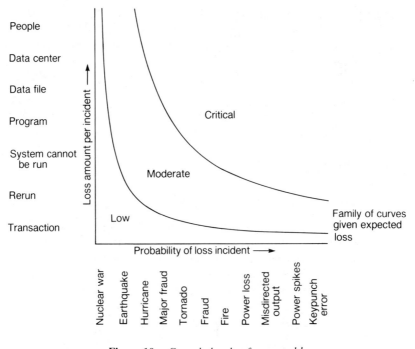

Figure 10. *Sample levels of expected loss*

What Are the Odds
That the Red Sea Will Part?

It is 1446 B.C. You are the commanding general of the Egyptian army. Pharaoh has directed you to pursue Moses and the Israelites and bring them back. As a good commander, you do your planning and consider the risks and the precautions (or controls) you need for a successful campaign. Your staff analyzes the data available and comes to you with expected loss information so you can finalize plans. You know you have some free thinkers, but one suggestion seems ridiculous: "We need boats because the Red Sea might part to allow the Israelites to escape, but not remain parted as we pursue them."

What is your response? Yes, the loss would be great—but the probability of its happening? No way! It has never happened before. I know we didn't plan for all those plagues, and that was a mistake; we have had plagues before and should have factored that into our analysis. But, the Red Sea? It has never parted, and there is no need even to think about it.

security, safety, internal audit, risk management, insurance, and controller, but also from user departments and quality assurance personnel. The important factors are: who is the first to know about losses, who is affected by losses, and who is responsible for correcting loss situations.

Dealing with Uncertainty

As we mentioned earlier, one of the problems with the formal risk assessment process (and the risk management process in general) is dealing with probabilities of events—dealing with uncertainty. Dealing with uncertainty is a real, and sometimes emotion-charged problem, as the Red Sea example demonstrates.

The Red Sea example illustrates a common problem in business organizations. Managers seldom consider events—especially loss events—for which they have no personal experience. Even when reasonably good industry data are available, if a certain event has not occurred in the organization, managers tend to feel that it never will. This attitude tends to bias the security and control decision process. Various approaches are possible in considering the odds that the Red Sea will part again. If you were the Egyptian general who replaced the one drowned in the Red Sea campaign, what should your response be?

1. I don't believe it ever happened and don't think it ever will. Our army simply lost the battle and needed an excuse. The experience data are wrong. No boats are needed.
2. I believe it happened, but don't believe it could ever happen again. The experience data are valid, but ignore them. No boats are needed.
3. I believe it happened and that it might happen again. The experience data are good and we will use them. Bring along a few boats.
4. I believe it happened and it is so fresh in my memory that I think it will happen again. The experience data are good, and we must protect against the event at all costs. Bring along boats for every soldier and for all our equipment.

Managers can adopt and justify each of these approaches and make decisions accordingly. One manager justified taking approach 2 by saying, "If it happens, I will probably be retired by then."

CASE STUDY

Background

☐ A large bank retained a loss control consulting firm to work with its EDP audit department on an EDP risk assessment. Although the consultant requested that the team include some users and staff from data processing, this proved not to be possible.

Method

The four consultants on the team included two computer security specialists, one engineer with a security background, and one decision analysis specialist. The four client members on the team were all from EDP audit, two of whom had significant experience in the EDP department. After some informal training, joint planning, and setting the scope of the project, the team performed a short risk assessment.

The team established strict bounds, with the following major assumptions:

1. Only one application was considered.
2. Data coming into the application were assumed to be accurate.
3. Once output left data processing it was not considered.

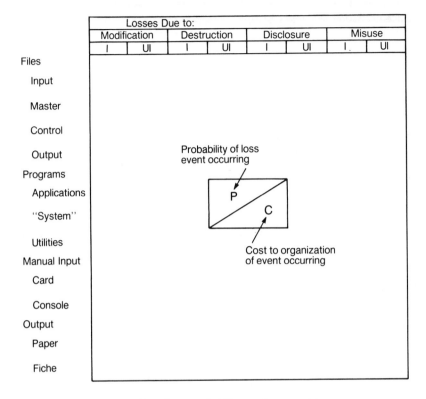

Figure 11. *Loss probability and cost matrix*

4. Physical and environmental threats were not included.
5. The operating system was not considered.
6. All hardware was assumed to work properly.

Figure 11 shows the resultant matrix. The vertical dimension (rows) was defined by objects or assets that could be lost—files, programs, manual input, and output. The horizontal dimension was defined by types of losses—modification, destruction, disclosure, and misuse—through both intentional and unintentional events. The elements of the matrix were to be pairs of values determined in the analysis—probabilities and loss amounts.

The actual development of data, the actual filling of the matrix, was the most intensive part of the project. All team members worked collectively, discussing each element and attempting to reach agreement on each value. A secretary recorded comments, reasons, assumptions, and occasionally a minority report for all entries made.

Table 1. *Scales for input values*

Probability of Occurrence (P)		Cost of Occurrence (C)	
Code	Rate	Code	$ Value
2	2 times/week	0	1
1	1 time/month	1	10
0	1 time/year	2	100
−1	1 time/10 years	3	1,000
−2	1 time/100 years	4	10,000
−3	1 time/1000 years	5	100,000
		6	1,000,000

Table 2. *Summary of basic results*

Probabilities		Cost		Expected Loss	
Per Year	Number	$ Per Event	Number	$ Value	Number
100	3	1	2	0.001	2
10	9	10	13	0.01	2
1	12	100	16	0.1	3
0.1	28	1,000	26	1	3
0.01	18	10,000	12	10	19
0.001	4	100,000	3	100	21
		1,000,000	2	1,000	12
				10,000	8
				100,000	3
				1,000,000	1

As a result of the initial assumptions, about one-sixth of the elements of the matrix were left blank by definition; that is, either the probability or the cost was believed to be zero or the item simply did not apply. For example, intentional disclosure of an input console was not considered a loss.

The values of the data pairs were set up on an order-of-magnitude scale and coded for easier bookkeeping. A logarithmic scale was established to facilitate development of input values. Using a range of an order of magni-

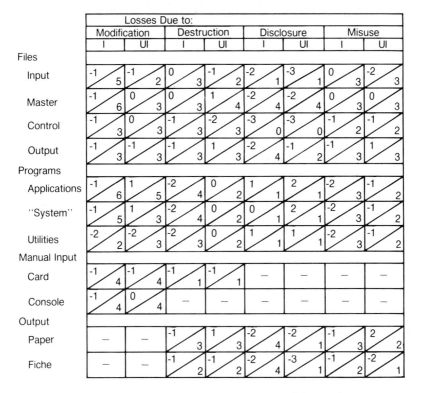

	Losses Due to:							
	Modification		Destruction		Disclosure		Misuse	
	I	UI	I	UI	I	UI	I	UI
Files								
Input	-1/5	-1/2	0/3	-1/2	-2/1	-3/1	0/3	-2/3
Master	-1/6	0/3	0/3	1/4	-2/4	-2/4	0/3	0/3
Control	-1/3	0/3	-1/3	-2/3	-3/0	-3/0	-1/2	-1/2
Output	-1/3	-1/3	-1/3	1/3	-2/4	-1/2	-1/3	1/3
Programs								
Applications	-1/6	1/5	-2/4	0/2	1/1	2/1	-2/3	-1/2
"System"	-1/5	1/3	-2/4	0/2	0/1	2/1	-2/3	-1/2
Utilities	-2/2	-2/3	-2/3	0/2	1/1	1/1	-2/3	-1/2
Manual Input								
Card	-1/4	-1/4	-1/1	-1/1	—	—	—	—
Console	-1/4	0/4	—	—	—	—	—	—
Output								
Paper	—	—	-1/3	1/3	-2/4	-2/1	-1/3	2/2
Fiche	—	—	-1/2	-1/2	-2/4	-3/1	-1/2	-2/1

Figure 12.   *Input values in the loss probability and cost matrix*

tude helped the team come to agreement on many of the probability values and cost values. Table 1 shows the scales and codes for each data item. To calculate the expected loss for each pair the following equation was used with the codes:

$$L = 10^{(P + C)}$$

Results

After developing all the data points and calculating the expected losses, the team performed a limited analysis. Figure 12 shows some of the input values in the loss probability and cost matrix. Table 2 summarizes the basic results—the frequency of probabilities, costs, and expected losses. The sum of the expected losses ($1,394,293) represents a total expected loss per year for the application in question.

Conclusions

The project provided the following important lessons:

1. Lack of input and analysis from data processing staff hampered efforts. The team had to make educated guesses about information that might otherwise have been available.
2. The process helped team members develop a much better understanding of risks and cost implications.
3. Although taking notes during the data development step required extra effort, the notes helped the team refine values and maintain consistency.
4. The limited scope made the process possible. Although initially the team had thought the limits too conservative, they were barely sufficient to make the task feasible.
5. A number of important or critical assets and threats were identified for the first time. The total expected loss value was determined but was not considered as useful or as meaningful as the identification of important areas.
6. Because time was limited, the team was able to develop only a preliminary analysis. Raw data were available for the more detailed analysis necessary to justify the project. □

Test the Quality of EDP
Risk Management Decisions in Your Organization

1. What would the impact on your organization be if your computer facility were totally inoperative for 1, 2, 5, 10 or 30 days? Estimate your mean-time-to-belly-up. Pick out the two or three application systems whose unavailability would be felt most. Which of the nine types of exposures in figure 3 would result? Are any of these "must control" situations? Investigate what preventative and corrective controls exist to reduce the likelihood of loss of computer services.

2. Select an application system that handles one of your more valuable assets. List several threats to that asset and estimate the probability of each threat occuring. Estimate the value of the asset and apply the formula from the section on risk assessment to calculate an expected loss. Consider the result. Is it reasonable? Large? Surprisingly large? Small?

How much would you pay to reduce the expected loss—50 percent? 90 percent? How might the money be spent to buy more controls?

3. In the discussion on the Red Sea, four possible attitudes and actions were listed:

a. Data are wrong—ignore them and do nothing.
b. Data are right—ignore them and do nothing.
c. Data are right—take limited precautions.
d. Data are right—take full precautions.

Find examples of each of these in your organization's response to some EDP threat. What are the data? What is the response? What is the rationale for the response? Are unacceptable risks involved?

The unhappy demon shows one of the consequences of defining responsibilities in an arbitrary manner. (From "Frank and Ernest," by Bob Thaves. Reprinted by permission. Copyright © 1978 NEA, Inc.)

4

Define Control Responsibilities

We must now consider both the allocation of control responsibilities among the various players and functions in the loss control process, and the bases for that allocation.

The Players

Because security and control are people issues, all members of an organization play some role in loss control. Organizations with strong loss control programs recognize this fact and use it to their advantage. Instilling a positive attitude toward security and control and promoting adherence to control procedures throughout the entire organization through corporate policy, the cooperation of senior management, education, and other deterrents can be much more cost effective than reacting to even one or two EDP-related losses. Although each person plays an important part in an effective loss control environment, a few organizational functions constitute the core of the program. These include the board of directors (especially the audit committee), senior management, EDP department management (operations and systems development), and internal audit (both financial and EDP). Also very much involved are external audit, users, quality assurance, personnel and legal departments, corporate security, risk management, computer security, and each member of the organization that affects or is affected by EDP.

General Issues

Several general issues must be addressed in a discussion of roles and responsibilities.

Clarity of definition: Most important is to define clearly the roles and responsibilities of each player. This reduces the tendency to manage loss control by reacting after the fact and finger-pointing. It also helps ensure that security and control activities, which are not usually "operations-critical"—the organization can probably continue to function without them—are not overlooked or allowed to fall dormant. Finally, well-defined roles ensure that the many different departments with important security and control roles will interact without overlap, gaps, or conflicting efforts.

Top-down approach: Roles and responsibilities should be defined and assigned from the top down, starting with the audit committee of the board of directors and senior management, and subordinate levels defined to support and implement directions from above. This approach should be continued through all levels until each member of the organization understands his or her responsibilities.

Periodic reinforcement: For most of the staff in an organization, loss control responsibilities represent only part of their job and may receive only secondary consideration. Periodic reinforcement provides recognition of responsibility. The easiest forms of reinforcement are training and personal development. Personnel who have primary responsibility for loss control (such as EDP audit and computer security) should receive direct training; they can then train others (such as user line management).

A more painful method of reinforcement is to enforce compliance and follow up loss control policies by imposing sanctions on those who violate organizational rules or laws. One troublesome problem in the area of computer abuse is that organizations often do not bring charges against staff who may have committed a computer-related crime. The rationale is that significant negative publicity may cause additional loss and embarrassment to the organization.

Constructive interaction: In practice, some of the players responsible for loss control activities may have differing operational objectives and may not interact constructively. Their behavior may range from lack of cooperation, to inaction, to agreeing to disagree, to outright antagonism. For example, in some organizations the audit department is viewed as a police force out to "get" others. An EDP auditor in such an organization will face considerable difficulties in helping system developers define controls. Users, developers, and auditors (to name the prime candidates) should make every effort to establish constructive relationships, and management should set an appropriate example. It is reasonable to include constructive interaction in statements of responsibilities.

Competence: The surest way to undermine a loss control program is to permit incompetence. Loss control actions and recommendations that are unrealistic, ineffective, or not cost effective lead in turn to lack of confidence in management and in the program. An individual assigned a responsible role must have demonstrated competence to perform the assigned tasks. Formal and on-the-job training, education, and apprenticeships can build and maintain competence.

Roles and Responsibilities

The audit committee of the board of directors: The audit committee of the board of directors has an important though somewhat unusual role in loss control: it has a well-defined supervisory responsibility but no direct operational ones. The functions of the audit committee should be recognized and well established and should command the respect of senior management through demonstrated involvement in control and audit activities. In many organizations the internal audit department has a strong reporting relationship to the audit committee together with a "dotted-line" relationship, for administrative purposes, to a senior corporate officer. When practice follows form, this usually proves to be the most productive arrangement: internal audit has the influence and independence it needs and the audit committee has an excellent source of loss control information.

The most important responsibilies of the audit committee are to review audit plans, to oversee internal audit department activities as evidenced by its reports, and to ask questions such as the following:

- What are the EDP loss implications of this control weakness?
- What are the major vulnerabilities in the organization's computer center and systems development process?
- Does EDP audit have the necessary expertise, resources, and access to areas of interest?
- Is the organization complying with SEC regulations and federal laws (and are we, as members of the board, exposing ourselves to potential liabilities)?

Responsibilities of the Audit Committee
of the Board of Directors

- Review the EDP audit program on a yearly basis.
- Review the EDP audit long term plan.
- Ensure that adequate resources are available to EDP audit.
- Ask questions of EDP audit.
- Review EDP audit reports.
- Suggest specific loss control measures.
- Request EDP loss control reviews.
- Exercise functional management control of EDP audit.

These basic responsibilities can lead to additional steps such as reviewing other internal audit reports for correlation, suggesting specific loss control measures, or initiating studies by internal audit, an in-house task force, or external organizations. The objective of such a study could be to produce an overall control evaluation of the EDP environment or to review in depth a particular area or problem. Concerned and active audit committees often initiate very useful projects of this kind. As with other actions, the board should respect the responsibilities or prerogatives of senior management without defaulting on legitimate responsibility or stifling concerns.

Another important responsibility is to review the EDP audit program on both a yearly and a long-term (three-to-five-year) basis. The objective of these reviews is to ensure that areas of concern to the audit committee are being addressed, that the scope of the reviews will be comprehensive and will meet the needs of the organization, and that adequate resources are made available to the audit function.

Senior management: The senior management of an organization has ultimate responsibility for EDP loss control as for all other functions. When senior management does not fully understand the implications and mechanisms involved in EDP loss control, it tends to abdicate responsibility to lower levels. Accepting the responsibility primarily means setting high-level direction for loss control and supporting the program by allocating adequate resources. The best way to set high level direction is to establish an organization-wide loss control policy. In the case study presented in chapter 2, the cover letter explaining the policy and establishing its authority was signed by the president and chairman of the board. Extracts from this letter follow:

The senior management of the Bank, by issuing this statement of policy, emphasizes as its ongoing and vital responsibility to the member local banks to preserve and safeguard the assets of this organization. The concept of providing a completely secure banking environment would entail the closure of all facilities and a cessation of business operations, and for that reason is unattainable and, moreover, unacceptable. It is therefore incumbent upon a prudent and concerned management to establish the framework for subsequent procedures and guidelines

---

Responsibilities of Senior Management

Major Responsibilities

- Accept ultimate responsibility.
- Provide high-level direction through corporate-wide policy.
- Ensure allocation of adequate resources.

Other Responsibilities

- Listen to subordinates and take interest when they report on loss control.
- Learn about loss control by attending seminars and interacting with managers from other organizations.
- Get outside advice or assistance when needed (when you get conflicting reports, when losses are too high, or when you believe you are operating under high risks).
- Set an example, such as observing your own control rules: wear your badge.
- Be open to ideas and take the advice you have requested when you have decided it is sound. ■ A counter example of this principle occurred when consultants were presenting the findings and recommendations of a study to the senior management of a large bank. Most of the executives listened and asked insightful questions. One, however, focused on a minor point, refused to accept the idea put forth, and interfered with moving the discussion on to other, more important issues.
- Ask questions of EDP audit and the computer security officer.
- Resist cutting back on EDP controls during economic downturns.
- If you request a loss control study, try to write the charter, scope, and objectives yourself.
- Think about your attitude toward risk: how much are you willing to lose, at what point does the company stop?
- Do not accept answers without evaluating them, especially if they are expressed in quantitative terms.
- When interacting with a consultant, listen, ask hard questions, and evaluate the advice from your business perspective.
- Put yourself into a control-oriented frame of mind and then do what you do best—analyze, make decisions, and allocate resources.

which, considering the requirements of the operating environment, seek to recognize and mitigate the potential for short- or long-term impact upon the availability of these assets to the Bank . . . .

The senior management of the Bank therefore considers this loss control policy to form an essential part of the overall policy framework on the Bank. We will initiate and/or maintain those measures which provide for the maximum security and utility for the respective categories of Bank assets, consistent with the operational requirements of the organization, and when the components of the policy can be determined to be cost effective within a reasonable time frame.

■ Another example of strong action by senior management occurred in a major U.S. petroleum company. The executive vice president of operations directed that a task force be established to evaluate the EDP loss control posture of the company. The executive himself carefully defined the charter

---

Responsibilities of Users

- Accept ownership of the application and the data.
- Do not default responsibility.
- Define needs and production requirements for the application.
- Define control needs on a business level (such as exception reports and control totals) but not on a technical level.
- Justify the development and use of the system.
- Be involved to an appropriate depth in all steps of the systems development life cycle.
- Consult with control experts if necessary (EDP auditor, external auditor, or outside consultant).
- Do not accept technical arguments from EDP that you do not understand.
- Use controls or get rid of them. ■ (If badges are required in your area insist that everybody wear them or do not have the badges at all.)
- Speak up when asked about control needs.
- Be realistic when evaluating the importance of your area, particularly when estimating potential losses and helping to establish a disaster recovery plan.
- Establish EDP expertise on your staff. ■ (A state agency hired a person with EDP knowledge and experience with the agency function to serve as a liaison with EDP, defining specifications and testing changes).
- Participate in developing test plans and in conducting tests of new systems and all system changes. Do not accept systems unless they meet *your* specifications.
- Formally sign off when accepting a system. Do not sign off if the system is not controlled as you desire.
- Have patience; accept the fact that it takes time to develop effective and well-controlled systems.
- Understand that controls cost money and require effort to implement.

---

and objectives for the task force and demonstrated considerable loss control insight and knowledge of internal corporate functions. This interest and insight showed the members of the task force that the vice-president was serious and would follow up on their recommendations.

Users: The primary responsibility of a user organization is to function as the owner of the application systems that support the business function. Ownership of EDP systems is a difficult concept that has grown out of data security concerns. The owner is responsible for the accuracy, validity, and maintenance of data; too often this responsibility passes by default to the EDP department. Even though EDP builds and operates systems, delivers output, and may even have influenced the design and technology to be incorporated, it is not the owner. Rather, its relation to the systems is custodial. User management must accept this responsibility; they, not EDP, are held accountable for the business results of the function.

From a loss control perspective, ownership responsibility means defining the control needs of the application. It also means providing information (as accurate as possible) about the relative importance of the application and the potential impact of its nonexecution—that is, what the organization would lose if there were an EDP disaster and the application could not be run.

EDP systems development: From a loss control perspective, the primary responsibility of EDP systems development is to handle the technical incorporation of controls in application systems. Those performing the design and analysis need to ensure that controls meet both the requests of users and

---

Responsibilities of
EDP Systems Development

- Perform the technical development and implementation of controls requested by the users: interpret user needs, define the requirements to meet those needs, implement the system and its controls, and test the system.
- Follow the systems development methodology as defined.
- Allocate sufficient resources to accomplish the task.
- Read *The Mythical Man Month* by Frederick P. Brooks, Jr. (Reading, Mass.: Addison-Wesley, 1975).
- Do *not* take defaulted responsibility for controls.
- Use development tools such as a program library maintenance package and a project tracking system.
- Talk to EDP audit.
- Produce usable and readable system documentation.
- Review chapter 8 on systems development.

Responsibilities of
EDP Quality Assurance

- Assist in developing control guidelines and standards based on general control objectives.
- Monitor the quality of systems developed through participation in the systems development life cycle.
- Develop or acquire tools to help developers. ■ (A variety of tools are being marketed to assist developers. One such package is called "The Programmer's Workbench.")
- Ensure that systems have built-in efficiency and effectiveness.
- Establish the department to be semi-independent so that it can both evaluate and act in a consulting mode.
- Establish the department at a reporting level at or above development teams so that it has sufficient authority.
- Act as a control consultant.

---

technical EDP needs. Those performing the actual coding and testing need to implement the specified controls accurately and test them sufficiently to ensure that they will work as expected.

This responsibility is actually a dual concern: first, that controls built into the application systems function with integrity; second, that the development (and change control process) occur in a controlled way. The second area addresses the historical problem that systems development generally takes longer and requires more resources than originally planned. The main tool providing control for these concerns is the systems development methodology, discussed at length in chapter 8.

EDP quality assurance: If the development effort of an organization is large enough, an EDP quality assurance (QA) department can serve a valuable role in the loss control process. It should address the quality of the application systems produced by the development organization, monitor adherence to organizational standards, and ensure adequate and proper testing of systems. The objectives and responsibilities of a quality assurance department resemble those of EDP audit. The stronger an organization's quality assurance function, the less need there is for expertise and effort from EDP audit.

Recent interest in QA functions has led to the establishment of an organization oriented exclusively to quality assurance: the Quality Assurance Institute, located at 9222 Bay Point Drive, Orlando, Florida.

Responsibilities of EDP Operations

- Help define technical operations controls.
- Implement operations controls.
- Execute production and operation controls.
- Check all input from users to verify that it is complete and properly defined by the users. Check all output to users to verify that it has been processed correctly from an EDP perspective.
- Serve as a custodian while user-owned data are in the EDP environment.

EDP operations: The EDP operations group is responsible for the day-to-day operation of the computer center and thus for the execution of application systems. Its primary loss control responsibilities are to design operational controls and to execute them on a continuing basis. The group must design not only general controls that deal with the operation of the computer center and apply to all application systems, but also controls that are unique to specific application systems. For the latter the operations group should interact with the systems development team to ensure that the controls needed are reasonable and are included in the design.

To meet the general control responsibility, an input/output control group usually serves as a liaison with user departments. This group accounts for all input data and performs basic balancing tests to ensure that all the data have been processed, accounted for, and included in the output.

EDP operations also serve as a custodian of data. The data and the programs that process the data are owned by users. However, while the data are being stored, retrieved, processed, or modified in the EDP environment, they are under the control of EDP. Thus responsibility for protection, backup, and recovery in the event of destruction falls to EDP operations.

Internal audit and EDP audit: Internal audit has one of the most important roles in loss control. It is an independent review function, operating as a service to management and a management control. EDP audit performs reviews and makes recommendations to strengthen the control process.

To move the organization from a reactive mode of loss control to a preventive and deterrent mode, EDP audit must concentrate on systems development. This means it must assume responsibility for helping produce control standards and guidelines and for reviewing the development process and specific development efforts.

Responsibilities of Internal Audit

- Work with others to define an audit program for the systems development life cycle, that is, specific audit steps with well-defined objectives, deliverables, and sign-off points.
- Audit the systems development process.
- Audit specific application systems.
- Audit computer centers.
- Report specific findings and recommendations to appropriate management.
- Respond to requests by the audit committee of the board of directors.
- Act constructively.
- Suggest control improvements when opportunities arise.
- Sign off on each step of the systems development life cycle. Define exactly what the sign-off means.
- Help develop control guidelines for EDP developers, being careful to maintain sufficient detachment from the implementation, thus preserving the ability to evaluate the controls independently.
- Develop and use control objectives in executing audit programs.

A less tangible but equally important responsibility is to act in a constructive mode. In many organizations, the audit department performs adequate reviews but in an adversary mode. (Some EDP auditors believe that they are evaluated by the number of critical findings they produce.) Every effort should be made to build a positive, constructive working relationship between audit and the EDP functions.

Personnel and legal departments: The personnel and legal departments play supporting roles in loss control. Their responsibilities are relatively minor but can be effective in alerting EDP areas to new laws and regulations that need to be observed or prepared for. Having an early warning system can prevent costly reaction to laws and regulations. Although few strong privacy and data confidentiality laws apply directly to commercial organizations, changes in these laws are possible. Guidance from personnel and legal staff on the development of any system that has a data base of information on individuals can help the organization avoid extensive reprogramming.

Corporate security: Although EDP accounts for a relatively minor part of its activity, the corporate security department is 100 percent oriented to loss control. When corporate security management has sufficient technical expertise in EDP to supervise the function effectively, it is advisable for the computer security department to report to corporate security. Until such a

Responsibilities of
Personnel and Legal Departments

- Review the design of systems for conformance to privacy laws and applicable privacy laws.
- Develop pre-employment screening policies and procedures, including the important issue of use of polygraph tests.
- Help set up an ethics policy and code of conduct specifically for EDP or incorporate EDP-related issues in corporate-wide policies.
- Encourage enlightened management by conducting training seminars, monitoring staff morale, and consulting with individual managers.
- Suggest controls (such as personnel policies and an employee code of conduct) that will serve as deterrents to undesirable staff behavior.

Responsibilities of Corporate Security

- Investigate intentional acts causing losses such as fraud and theft by interacting with external groups and directing in-house investigations.
- Monitor controls (such as exception reports for physical access to computer centers.)
- Function as a technical resource.
- Manage the guard staff that controls access to computer facilities and areas in which EDP staff operate.
- Perform crisis management and serve as a coordinator in an emergency (such as a fire or civil disruption) to initiate and organize safety and recovery actions.

- Manage the computer security function if it is organized to report to corporate security.
- Assist with pre-employment screening.
- Serve on EDP loss control committees, task forces, and projects even if you have no technical expertise. These efforts provide an excellent opportunity to learn about EDP from others.
- Help define, manage the installation of, and monitor the physical protection of the computer center facilities.
- Interact with the insurance department regarding EDP loss coverage.
- Maintain control of the corporate security manual and, if appropriate, the computer security manual. ■ In one organization the corporate security department maintained the manual on a word processor. The only full copy was the machine-readable version. Other departments received only the sections that were required for their functions.
- Learn about computers, EDP operations, and computer people.

Responsibilities of
the Insurance Department

- Analyze, advise management on, and manage EDP insurance coverage.
- Analyze EDP-related risks throughout the organization.
- Assist with efforts to quantify EDP-related risks.

---

relationship can be fully developed, computer security should report within the EDP organization, preferably to its senior executive.

A very subtle but important responsibility is to serve on any group that is reviewing EDP loss control. In this context the role of corporate security is not to supply EDP expertise but to serve as a liaison on security issues between EDP and the rest of the organization. Many organizations have found that this form of participation improves coordination among groups and that recommendations tend to be more pragmatic.

Insurance department: Because EDP facilities represent a significant direct investment, insurance plays an important role in EDP loss control. The insurance department can be very useful in helping analyze how to handle risks to EDP assets. The cost of insurance coverage is precise and gives management a specific alternative to spending money for controls that may prevent or reduce insurable risks.

Some organizations have broadened the scope and responsibility of the insurance department to include computer security. Theoretically this reporting structure appears to be effective, for it provides both independence from operations and a fuller orientation to security and loss control. However, there has been insufficient industry experience to confirm this theory.

Computer security: The computer security department, the keystone of EDP loss control, acts as a monitor and consultant for all aspects of loss control in the EDP environment. The two accompanying examples present a job description and responsibility statement for computer security functions in two financial organizations.

Job Description—Computer Security Officer

Title: Computer Security Officer

Reports to: Manager, Data Processing Operations

Purpose of position: To provide for the implementation and monitoring of security-related policies and guidelines with the System Management Division. These policies relate to both physical and data security issues.

Responsibilities of Computer Security

- Help develop systems development guidelines and standards.
- Participate in the systems development process.
- Act as a control consultant.
- Monitor unauthorized access to files, misuse of passwords, exception reports, and major software problems.
- Lead EDP loss control projects such as disaster recovery planning, implementation of an access control package, and the development of an organization-wide EDP loss control policy.
- Serve as an EDP loss control coordinator.
- Collect data on, summarize, and report EDP-related losses.
- Plan, assist in the development of, and maintain the organization's EDP security or loss control manual.
- Provide EDP loss control training and education.
- Assist the security department in EDP-related investigations.

Duties and responsibilities:

- Establish guidelines in support of policies for information control and security. This will be accomplished in conjunction with other involved areas including Data Administration, Data Base Administration, Technical Support, Quality Assurance, Applications Systems Development, and Internal Audit, and with management approval. This will involve implementation, administration, and monitoring of the security facilities provided for use with the system software, including password administration, access level authorizations, and command level authorizations.
- Implement and monitor policies affecting information control and security.
- Provide security for computer-readable and computer-processed data.
- Update and ensure adequacy of disaster plans, backup and recovery, and file retention schedules.
- Establish, in conjunction with operations management and internal audit (and with management approval), policies and guidelines for security in operational procedures in the computer operating areas.

Responsibility Statement
Systems Security Section

This section is responsible for corporate-wide planning, monitoring, and coordinating the implementation of procedures to insure the security and reliability of the Bank's data processing operating environment.

1. Plan, recommend, and coordinate the development and implementation of security procedures related to the physical access and environmental control systems.

a. Plan for and provide control of physical access to the Bank's data processing facilities.

b. Plan for and monitor environmental safeguards for the data processing facilities, such as the fire detection and suppression systems, alternate or uninterruptible power supplies, physical communication paths, heating, ventillating, and air conditioning.

2. Develop and maintain the Bank's EDP systems security manual containing security-related policies, standards, guidelines, and operating procedures.

3. Design and exercise disaster recovery plans that will sustain critical system services in the event of a catastrophic failure in the data processing operations.

   a. Develop systems and procedures for the preservation, integrity, security, and backup of critical data and programming files.

   b. Develop and maintain the Bank's EDP disaster recovery manual containing detailed information about the procedures to be used in the case of a major disruption.

4. Support line management, auditors, user departments, personnel, and staff in carrying out their security-related responsibilities.

   a. Develop awareness of the security responsibilities of personnel, using appropriate training programs.

   b. Advise management on the assignment of line management responsibility for implementing the security policy.

   c. Support internal and external auditors in their periodic reviews to assure that security policies and standards are being complied with and recommend enhancements in these areas.

   d. Provide the necessary EDP security support to line management in the performance of their responsibilities.

   e. Review new systems during their development to become familiar with these systems before their implementation and make security an intrinsic part of the system design and maximize the effectiveness of security facilities. All systems must have the approval of Systems Security as a condition for acceptance of a completed system design.

   f. Review production systems periodically to ensure that security objectives established during development have been met and maintained.

   g. Provide a channel for the exchange of security information among legal, auditing, user, and EDP management.

   h. Recommend changes to production systems to implement enhanced security features for the purposes of loss control, monitoring, and reporting.

5. Maintain state-of-the-art knowledge of computer security practices, products, and legislation.

   a. Maintain a continuing review of existing and proposed state and federal legislation and regulations pertaining to information systems security and privacy. Keep management aware of the regulatory changes that will affect information privacy, information processing, and all security standards and techniques.

   b. Continually review and evaluate security alternatives to determine courses of action based upon technical implications, knowledge of business objectives, and established policies.

    c. Evaluate the need for encryption techniques and other devices to protect the integrity and security of the Bank's data.

    d. Report to senior management from time to time on the state of security of the Bank's data processing facilities.

    e. Plan for and coordinate the corrective and preventive program of actions necessary to improve security and reliability on a continuous basis.

    f. Maintain close contact with persons with similar responsibilities in other corporations and professional organizations to keep up-to-date with the generally accepted practices in the field.

6. Plan, recommend, and coordinate the development and implementation of access to the Bank's data processing resources such as data, programs, terminals, transactions, and commands.

    a. Recommend EDP systems, including hardware and software that could be used principally for a security application.

    b. Administer access control systems including the generation, issuance, distribution, and maintenance of user IDs, passwords, and keys. The responsibility and authority may be assigned to other areas if it is not possible to conveniently administer the controls due to limitations in hardware, software, or access to a particular resource.

7. Monitor compliance with and report variances from established security practices and procedures.

    a. Monitor the use of all computer facilities to detect and act upon unauthorized access and use.

    b. Develop and implement a management system to measure and report performance against the established standards and procedures.

    c. Manage the development of procedures for detecting, reporting, and investigating breaches in computer security, and with the assistance of appropriate security and auditing personnel direct the investigation of security breaches.

8. Manage the Systems Security Section staff and other related activities.

    a. Determine special resource requirements such as manpower, training, and equipment, and develop plans, schedules, and cost data relative to various security responsibilities.

    b. Set objectives for future development of security systems.

Each member of the organization: Each member of an organization is responsible for being aware of EDP loss control and for adhering to the

---

General Responsibilities

- Adhere to security and control policies.
- Adhere to code of ethics and standards of conduct.
- Report loss control infractions.
- Report loss control problems.

---

established policies and procedures. This includes any code of ethics or standards of conduct adopted by the organization.

One control that deserves special attention is the reporting of control violations, especially for staff members not having direct security and loss control responsibility. Reporting infractions by outsiders is normally not a problem. However, reporting a violation by a co-worker or challenging someone unknown to the staff member is generally not done in our society. It is much more realistic to expect staff to report problems rather than people.

CASE STUDY

Background

☐ A high-technology company in a very rapidly growing industry had had an average annual growth rate of 35 percent over the past eight years. Its product was high in value and its manufacture very process-intensive. The company's success resulted from its making more and better products and getting them to market quickly and effectively. The company was a heavy user of EDP services; it operated two large-scale processors in its U.S. headquarters and one additional processor in each of its European and Asian factories.

In the first years, management had focused on production and marketing. As the organization matured, considerations broadened to include security. The company's product was small and easily concealable, the high rate of manufacturing scrappage provided a possible cover for theft, and there was a "gray" market in the product that could tempt employees to thievery.

The company adopted two parallel strategies. One was to strengthen conventional control of access to the product by tightening supervision of badging and physical access. The other was to develop and install a comprehensive raw material, work-in-process, and finished goods inventory control system. The EDP department was assigned the task of establishing the inventory system, some estimates were made as to when the new system would be available, and management breathed a sigh of relief and turned its attention to other pressing matters.

The decision to go ahead with the system design had been taken a few years ago, when the term *data base* conjured up dreams of elegant systems that would do just about anything for anybody. The EDP department saw the inventory system requirement as the vehicle to take the company from conventional systems to a future of integrated data base technology. Thus the very practical business need for an application system was allowed to be submerged beneath an attractive technical concept that, though valuable, should not have been an end in itself.

The EDP department did not consider security questions until well into development, and then initially only from the standpoint of protecting the inventory records from mischance. More sophisticated controls were added only subsequently. The corporate security department confined its attention to controlling physical access to the inventories of raw material, product, and work in process. Users in the manufacturing department were consulted on details of the process, but apparently neither manufacturing nor EDP seriously broached the issue of controls. As is often the case in rapidly growing companies, the internal audit department was stretched very thin; it had no EDP audit specialists, and could not contribute effectively to the control integrity of the system under development.

Method

The EDP department hired a data base expert and acquired a proprietary data base management package, chosen for its absolute technical merit rather than for how well it fitted the needs of the specific application of inventory control or how well it responded to the urgency of achieving some basic control over inventories. The fact that the expert was assigned as the project manager further confirmed the general perception that this was a research, rather than a business, project. Development proceeded slowly, users lost confidence that the new system would ever be fully available, and stopgap measures, both manual and computer-based, proliferated. Midway in the project EDP management became more alert to the issues of EDP loss control and appointed the project manager as EDP security manager in addition to his other duties.

Results

The inventory system took more than twice as long and cost twice as much to reach an operational state as the original estimate had forecast. No major inventory losses were detected during this period, so it is hard to say whether the problems associated with development cost the company anything directly, but it is clear that the excess costs of the development itself were only the floor under the real losses that the company experienced.

The corporate security department, however, developed considerable skill in EDP security matters during the course of the development. The inventory system project manager realized that he could not perform the additional duties of EDP security manager and allowed some of those responsibilities to devolve to corporate security: first physical access controls, then administration of user IDs and passwords for the terminal access to the computer facility. Next, corporate security assumed supervision of disaster planning and general information security matters. In the end, corporate security cross-trained some of its people in EDP and brought one professional in from the EDP department to operate a fully self-sufficient EDP security group.

Conclusions

Although there was no formal post-implementation audit, company management met several times and discussed the development project and its consequences. The general conclusions of these review sessions were:

- Management should have accepted more responsibility for promoting and reviewing the project.
- Users abrogated their responsibility for prescribing the controls needed in the inventory system.
- Users allowed themselves to be "snowed" by the EDP professionals on the technical issues relating to data base technology.
- EDP shirked its basic responsibility to respond primarily to user needs.
- Internal audit should have given at least a little time to control review and to review the project itself, especially because of the project's importance to the company as a whole.
- Corporate security learned slowly but solidly about the importance of EDP systems in the general loss control process, and applied its lessons by filling the EDP security gap through training and acceptance of security responsibility.
- The company was simply lucky that no major theft occurred while inventory control was weak. □

Analyzing Responsibilities
for EDP Loss Control
in Your Organization

1. Select one or more lists of responsibilities presented earlier in the chapter. Opposite each item write one or two sentences characterizing the degree to which that responsibility is carried out by the corresponding function in your organization.

2. Where substantial differences exist between our approach and the practice in your organization, answer the following questions:

    a. Does another department assume the responsibility? If so, is it appropriately placed there because of the special character of your organization? Would you recommend a change? If so, how should this change be made?

    b. If some other department is not assuming the responsibility, does this omission represent a vulnerability to EDP-related loss? If so, how can the vulnerability best be removed or reduced? How much priority is assigned to dealing with this vulnerability? What organizational steps, in terms of changed responsibility, are in order?

A Perspective on Chapter 5

> *Mr. Puckett is making the same mistake that many people do in working within an organization; he is reading his own interpretation into the statement of the organization's objectives. (From "Frank and Ernest," by Bob Thaves. Reprinted by permission. Copyright © 1978 NEA, Inc.)*

5

Support Organization-wide Control Standards

This chapter tells you how to translate corporate loss control objectives and strategies into real-world results in unequivocal ways, through control standards. It also emphasizes the importance of corporate-level support for those standards through constructive action.

Benefits

The development, installation, use, and enforcement of rules is one of the least sought-after jobs in any organization. Nevertheless, we believe control standards are one of the foundations of loss control. Proper organization-wide control standards provide four essential benefits: direction, effectiveness, uniformity, and measureability.

Direction: Organization-wide control standards provide guidance for the staff in dealing with the vital issues of security, control and auditability. Without a uniform, cohesive statement of management's views, each manager will apply her or his interpretation of what is appropriate in addressing these issues. Standards furnish guidance by specifying concisely and in simple terms how the staff should address the selection, implementation, and application of controls.

Effectiveness: Top management support for control standards ensures that the rank and file will take those standards seriously. Every organization mirrors the attitudes of its leaders. If control of EDP systems is left to be worked out as a special case by each systems analyst, little is likely to be accomplished. A set of control standards provides the basis and impetus for workable solutions to control needs by clearly defining the scope of the application of controls in the organization. Among other things, standards should specify (or at least suggest) a threshold: What is the asset limit below which it is no longer necessary to apply controls? How are assets to be defined— only as money and property and perhaps as data? Or is competitive position, for example, an asset to be subjected to controls?

Uniformity: A set of control standards that applies to the whole organization ensures a uniform approach to control issues and adherence to certain minimum standards. One of the most common failings security and control experts report is lack of uniformity of control. In identifying controls in application systems, they are likely to find one or two glaring weak spots and two or three "super-controls" in an application. The latter are often installed and operated at significant expense but are made useless by the weak spots.
■ For example, a major manufacturer put great effort into strengthening the check issuance controls in its new accounts payable system, only to find that false vendor names and false receiving documents were being entered through gaps in input controls in the new system.

Measurement: Finally, control standards provide a means of measuring achievement. ■ After passage of the Foreign Corrupt Practices Act, many companies, concerned about the act's provisions regarding controls, requested assessments of the adequacy of controls in their systems. Most of these companies had to depend on qualitative judgments because they lacked standards on which to base more precise assessments. Many chief executives came away from these assessments with the realization that they had no means in place for measuring the adequacy of controls, and thus no way of knowing how nearly they met the requirements of the act. Standards must specify how the effectiveness of controls is to be judged, who is responsible for gathering the data to make the judgments, and how the results are to be fed back to improve future performance. Management's objective in any business process is improvement; without measurement and loop closure the process is futile, even counterproductive.

As a corollary to the measurement objective, the internal audit department should be able to use the standards as norms by which to measure compliance or conformance. Today there are not enough "generally accepted" EDP standards. Many sets of checklists exist, but the profession has not reached the level of maturity that produces industry standards. This puts EDP auditors, and the enterprise itself, at a disadvantage. ■ Using a kind of twisted logic, in more than one instance auditors have cited lack of standards as a reason for not auditing the EDP department! Despite the lack so far of such standards, there are some straightforward concepts related to the prudent protection of the EDP function. These include the provision of backup files and facilities and of physical and terminal security. Expansion of these concepts into definitive standards will help provide the measurement benefit.

Management's Support Role

A set of corporate control standards that provides these four benefits deserves the support of an organization's managers. How can management participate in obtaining the objectives and use the standards in the ongoing business of the organization?

Chapters 1 and 2 discussed the primary importance of positive attitudes toward loss control and the formulation of a loss control program. Those proper attitudes are the fundamental influences shaping the content and style of the standards, and the loss control program is the context in which the standards are applied. Setting organization philosophy regarding the use of controls is the essential first phase of management's support role. It acknowledges management's basic responsibility to lead. Once established, the philosophy must be embodied in published standards. In the second phase of management's support role, the ongoing phase, four aspects are crucial:

- Support for good business practices
- Support for business integrity
- Support for conformance to laws and regulations
- Support for continuing assessment

A body of good business practices has been built up over the years by businesses and refined by knowledgeable managers. Schools and hands-on experience teach workers and managers these practices. Top management, suppliers, and customers all expect these practices to be used consistently and insightfully. Organization control standards should summarize the principles behind these practices and mandate their use.

Integrity has two related meanings: "uprightness" and "soundness." Both are applicable to management's support for controls. Because effective controls are one of the foundations of business integrity, and because control standards contribute fundamentally to the installation and operation of effective controls, management's support for these standards is support for business integrity. Viewed from the opposite perspective, the level of control effectiveness often defines (by default, if management does not take a positive role) the level of a business's integrity.

Management must also make it clear that standards exist to support conformance to government laws and regulations. After several business scandals in the 1970s, the Foreign Corrupt Practices Act and other, similar legislation were passed. Because the penalties for violation of that act can fall directly on the manager, this aspect of management's support role is all the more important.

The final aspect, support for continuing assessment of control standards, meets the obligation of every successful manager to measure the degree to which his or her planning, organization, and implementation have met company goals.

Thus management's support for control standards must take five forms: management establishes organization philosophy regarding the use of controls, addresses conformance to good business practices, establishes conformance to an organization-wide standard of integrity, affirms the absolute requirement to conform to law and regulation, and endorses the principle of measurement of the effectiveness of controls. Although it is the responsibility of supervisors to apply and enforce the detailed provisions of the standards, standards cannot be effective without active support from top management.

Content and Nature of Standards

Control standards affect not only the three aspects of the EDP activity—systems development, applications systems, and operations—but also, two important legal and regulatory areas, privacy laws and the Foreign Corrupt Practices Act. All five topics are important to the content and nature of standards.

Control standards are *not* a "laundry list" of possible controls. They are, rather, statements of principle in policy form. Several excellent books on controls, listed in the box below, exist for use by systems designers and users. However, they cannot serve as substitutes for a statement of organization policy on controls.

Standards for EDP systems development: Systems development begins with recognition of the need for an EDP system to perform a business function and continues through definition, design, coding, testing, conversion, maintenance, and enhancement to the end of the system's useful life, insofar as changes to the system configuration are concerned. In most enterprises today, about half of each EDP dollar is spent in systems development; so from a financial perspective it is certainly worthwhile to exercise some control. But more important is the impact of EDP systems on the business processes of the organization as a whole. The vast majority of accounting controls, for example, are implemented through EDP systems. Thus it is crucial that controls be built into these systems so that they have integrity and perform exactly as intended.

Selection of Specific Controls

The selection of specific controls is outside the scope of this book and generally beyond the technical skills and responsibility of most managers. Nevertheless, the following books can serve as valuable texts or references for managers or their subordinates who are especially interested in the topic.

These books offer both structure for the classification of controls and methodologies for control selection.

Eason, T. S.; See, M.E.; Russell, S.H.; FitzGerald, J. M.; and Ruder, B. *Systems Auditability and Control.* 3 vols. Altamonte Springs, Fla.: Institute of Internal Auditors, 1977.

FitzGerald, J. M. *Internal Controls for Computerized Systems.* Redwood City, Calif.: Jerry FitzGerald and Associates, 1978.

—. *Designing Controls into Computerized Systems.* Redwood City, Calif.: Jerry FitzGerald and Associates, 1981.

Mair, W. C.; Wood, D. R.; and Davis, K. W. *Computer Controls and Audit.* 2d ed. Altamonte Springs, Fla.: Institute of Internal Auditors, 1976.

A proper control is one that meets the criteria discussed in the preceding two sections. It supports conformance to good business practice, conformance to corporate integrity, conformance to law and regulation, and is inherently measurable in its effect. Further, it is applied with consistency and completeness across the system in which it resides and is also consistent with applications in other related systems. This is a tall order; but that should not deter management from establishing these criteria as performance targets for everyone involved in systems development.

Standards must address not only what kinds of controls should be used, but also how they get into systems. They must therefore state control objectives clearly in defining the system and assign responsibility for proposing, designing, and approving the controls. The EDP systems professional, EDP quality assurance person, and EDP auditor all have a role in this process, but the user plays the leading role. We discuss this topic in the section below, "How to Develop Control Standards."

Standards dealing with loss control in systems development must also provide control over the process itself, since it consumes substantial resources. Control standards should therefore outline or otherwise specify methodologies for technical and fiscal control of the development process. Again, the user, EDP auditor, and EDP quality assurance person participate along with the development staff itself. A well-run development process is based on well-defined phases, which produce predefined documentary products, usually referred to as deliverables. These products are reviewed according to established criteria and are individually costed and managed in terms of expenditure versus progress. Chapter 8 describes in detail some mechanisms for conducting and controlling the development process.

Finally, control standards for systems development must address the measurement of effectiveness, mandating some sort of post-implementation review of systems. The purpose is not punitive; the reviewer is interested not in *who* (if anyone) went wrong, but in *what* went right and wrong and how the developers can do as well or better next time. Such a review must research the ongoing system to evaluate how its controls work in the real world and what improvements, if any, are appropriate.

Standards for EDP application systems: Application systems are programs or a set of programs that serve some business purpose or solve some business problem. For example, the set of related programs that receive input from time cards, calculate payroll amounts, and produce checks, withholding-tax schedules, and the like can be considered an application system, or as it is often called, a payroll application. The ensemble of application systems used in the conduct of an organization's business usually represents a substantial investment. Furthermore, in most cases continued integrity and availability are vital to the survival of the enterprise; business transactions would be forced to a halt if the application systems became unavailable, substantially inoperative, or inaccurate. Thus EDP application systems, like the manual systems they replace or supplement, must have controls to assure their integrity, usefulness, and viability.

Properly structured EDP control standards address the ways in which controls in application systems are documented. In particular, a statement of control objectives is necessary to the efficient progress of the functional design process. Standards should require the formulation of such a statement early in the design. In addition, clear, easily identifiable, and straightforward descriptions of control mechanisms and techniques to be used in the application technical design are prerequisite to entering production usage of the system. Control standards should establish the requirements for these descriptions.

Standards must also address one of the auditor's basic jobs—verifying the presence and operability of controls in the application system. The standards should require documentation of the kind of controls, their precise location in the system, and the technique of implementation in the programs and procedures of the system. Simple tests should be provided as a part of the design to make the task of verifying operability easy and unequivocal.

Finally, standards should ensure that application controls are implemented in ways that cause them to report any attempts to circumvent them. The self-instrumentation of controls is of fundamental importance and is thus a proper subject for corporate standards.

Standards for EDP operations: EDP operations comprise all the activities associated with the production running of the organization's suite of application systems: the initial capture of data, point-to-point movement of data by communications, processing and storing data, and outputting data and distributing the output to its ultimate users. Controls for these operations must be general—that is, they must work for any application.

Control standards for EDP operations should address two general objectives: ensuring accuracy and completeness of processing, and ensuring the continued availability of the processing resource. To meet the first objective, standards should prescribe levels of accuracy and completeness. To meet the second, standards must set criteria for disaster planning, physical and data security, and safety. Standards should also set performance levels for verifying and assessing the effectiveness of controls.

Standards for conformance to privacy laws: The right to privacy is the right of the individual to protection against inappropriate or unnecessary exposure of personal information. In recent years, the ability of computers to handle large data bases and perform cross-correlations in those data bases has focused concern on issues related to privacy. Clearly, organization standards for control in EDP systems must deal with these issues. From a potpourri of state and federal laws and regulations some basic principles emerge that deserve attention. First, data bases should not be accumulated for ill-defined purposes or on the basis of ill-defined criteria. In the 1960s and early 1970s, for example, U.S. Army Intelligence assembled a data base of "malcontents and agitators." Congressional pressure caused this data base to be destroyed because the criteria for inclusion of private individuals were very loose and the purposes to which the data were put were suspect. As a corollary, data bases should be used only for the purpose for which they were assembled. The indiscriminate sale of mailing lists violates this principle. A few years ago, litigation restricted one state's freedom to sell its vehicle registration data base to automobile dealers and manufacturers. Thus, it appears that control standards embodying these principles are necessary and appropriate.

The second basic principle is that data bases containing personal data should be accessible for examination and correction by the people on whom they contain information. Personnel files within an organization and credit files in the business environment as a whole are the two most comprehensive examples. Organization control standards should support this principle by requiring that convenient means be available for examining and correcting computerized data bases.

Finally, the organization must accept full responsibility for the accuracy of all the data bases it maintains. This implies a responsibility to provide means for disinterested parties to verify, correct, and audit its data bases. The control standards should specify mechanisms for ensuring this access.

Standards for conformance to the Foreign Corrupt Practices Act: In the years following its enactment, the Foreign Corrupt Practices Act (FCPA) of 1977 and the Securities and Exchange Commission (SEC) regulations, promulgated to implement the FCPA, had a far-reaching impact on the control of EDP systems and processes (and accounting in general). Recently, concern has diminished somewhat, but the basic provisions of the act remain a significant influence on the nature, strength, and comprehensiveness of controls in EDP systems. Though designed to address certain unethical business practices used by U.S. firms in international dealings, it also applies to most domestic corporations, their managers, and directors. The act establishes personal liability, through both fines and imprisonment, for noncompliance; imposes fines on corporations for noncompliance; and permits civil suits by stockholders.

The FCPA is the first federal law to require that corporations:

1. Maintain adequate internal accounting controls.
2. Follow generally accepted accounting practices.
3. Maintain accurate books and records.
4. Provide for adequate reporting of financial conditions.
5. Have adequate internal or external audit overview to monitor compliance with the act.

Two provisions of the act have direct implications for loss control. The first requires corporations to "make and keep books, records and accounts, which, in reasonable detail, accurately and fairly reflect the transactions and

---

One Company's Experience with the FCPA

One multinational manufacturer of electronics equipment, sensitized to the possible consequences of nonconformance to the FCPA by concern over a small but possibly illegal payment in the early 1970s, initiated a far-reaching study of its accounting controls and the extent of their compliance with the act. The study was initiated by the audit committee of the board of directors and was conducted by the internal audit department, supported by a team of EDP consultants.

The results of the study reassured management and the board that accounting controls in the EDP systems were generally acceptable. By chance, the study coincided with a redesign of the company's financial applications for its European division. The attention generated by the study prompted careful controls review of the proposed new designs, and several worthwhile improvements in controls integrity were made early enough in the development process to keep the cost of the changes low and related delays minimal. As an added bonus, a small EDP-related fraud was uncovered in the purchasing area, and the ensuing recovery of losses paid for about 10 percent of the cost of the study.

---

dispositions of the assets of the issuer." The crucial word here is *accuracy.* Experts and court cases have generally interpreted it to involve the concept of materiality. In other words, the need for accuracy applies to material amounts only. However, what materiality means is not always completely clear. It is fairly certain that if the consequence of an inaccuracy is material, then so is the inaccuracy itself. It is also clear that illegal behavior is always material. Notwithstanding these difficulties of interpretation, control standards must address the issues of accuracy and materiality in ways sufficiently clear to provide reasonable guidance to the people responsible for designing and operating the organization's business EDP systems.

The second key provision requires corporations to "devise and maintain a system of internal accounting controls sufficient to provide reasonable assurances" that:

1. transactions are authorized
2. transactions are recorded
3. access to assets is controlled
4. assets and asset records are compared at regular intervals.

To be in compliance, a system of internal controls must exist, be functioning, and be effective. However, controls are required only if they are cost effective. This implies that management must make estimates and judgments and exercise prudence. The four requirements above are too broad to be used verbatim as control standards. "Providing reasonable assurances," for example, involves actions by senior managers, directors, operating managers, and auditors. The function of standards is to ensure that the appropriate people understand and perform the necessary actions. Three lists below, summarizing the actions we consider necessary, can serve as a basis for specific provisions in the standards.

Recommended FCPA Compliance Actions for Senior Managers and Directors

1. Establish policies and procedures to:
   - safeguard assets against loss
   - produce reliable financial records.
2. Understand the controls functions of record keeping and internal accounting.
3. Become aware of compromising control deficiencies.
4. Allocate resources for system and audit functions to:
   - investigate, report, and correct deficiencies
   - monitor compliance with established policies, procedures, and law.

Recommended FCPA Compliance Actions for Operating Managers

1. Implement corporate policies and procedures.
2. Review and document deficiencies in system control.

3. Implement adequate controls to correct existing deficiencies.
4. Design and implement new systems with adequate controls.
5. Work with internal and external auditors and consultants to help ensure compliance.
6. Evaluate cost-benefit and the practicality of proposed controls.
7. Educate staff about the purposes of and need for controls.

Recommended FCPA Compliance Actions for Auditors

1. Monitor compliance with existing policies and procedures.
2. Examine and report on control deficiencies in existing systems and systems under development.
3. Examine and report on errors and irregularities.
4. Examine and report on financial representations.
5. Recommend measures to improve controls.
6. Establish and sustain education and training programs for internal auditors.
7. Participate in establishing standards.

How to Develop Control Standards

Control standards demand careful development because they articulate the organization's policy and in turn can affect important aspects of the image, role, and operations of the enterprise. Many people inside and outside the organization will examine the standards carefully and guide or measure their actions by them.

Who should participate as doers and reviewers? Representatives from the EDP organization know the technology of information processing and the processes embodied in the application systems that make the business go. Internal audit must help develop the standards it has to live with and enforce, but its role must be restricted to general guidance, lest its independence be compromised by too deep an involvement. Representatives of the organizations using the applications systems should also contribute their knowledge of business processes to the development of the standards.

Depending on the knowledge and skills available within this group, it may be wise to add some input from outsiders with experience in developing standards. Three good sources of outside skills are external auditors, consultants, and outside members of the board of directors. These should serve as facilitators and reviewers, not as workers, to provide the most value and transfer the most skills to the inside group. Other reviewers should include the organization's executives, its in-house counsel, and its law firm. Table 3 lists these participants and their roles in the process of developing the standards, as described in the following paragraphs.

Table 3. *Participants and roles in the development of control standards*

Steps	Participants		
	Standards Team	*Facilitators/Reviewers*	*Final Reviewers*
	Systems Designers Quality Assurers Internal Auditors Users	External Auditors Consultants Outside Board Members	Executives House Counsel Outside Law Firm
1. Secure and assess model standards	Perform	Advise/support	—
2. Prepare standards	Perform		
Assign areas	Team leaders	—	—
Prepare drafts	Team members	Advise	—
Review drafts	—	Perform	
3. Achieve consensus	Perform		
Resolve differences	Team leaders	Advise/support	Participate as necessary
Write final draft	Team	Advise/support	
4. Obtain approval	Perform		
Prepare summary and presentation	Team leaders	Advise/support	—
Circulate/present	Team leaders	—	—
Approve	—	Recommend	Perform

The best starting point is a model that suits the organization's needs. If standards already exist in some form, check them for completeness against the model described in the section "Content and Nature of Standards." Existing control standards may not be labeled as such; some may exist in the EDP and accounting departments as internal documents, guidelines, or policies. Standards should exist for each of the categories outlined in the five subparagraphs of that section. If you are starting from scratch, use that section as the model and address each of the topics, establishing your own standards as you go and using the knowledge of group members as appropriate. Assign areas to specialists to work up in draft proposals, review the proposals in committee, achieve agreement, and work your way through the topic areas.

Once the working group is well on its way, pass completed sections around to the more constructive of your reviewers to get feedback quickly. Use the facilitators to help resolve disagreements. Outsiders with experience in other organizations can often cast a new light on the points in contention. They are also helpful in the role of quality assurers for the end product.

When the control standards are formulated to the working group's satisfaction, summarize them carefully, prepare a concise stand-up presentation, circulate the summary and the standards themselves to all your reviewers, and invite them to a formal presentation. Make the presentation, answer all the questions, and solicit their approval.

CASE STUDY

Background

☐ A major foreign bank was contemplating an extensive redesign of its applications systems, including all of its on-line counter service applications, and a substantial upgrading of the hardware configurations supporting those applications. Sensitized to the need by earlier work in the loss control area, bank management resolved to base the new systems development on a carefully planned set of control standards. Bank management formed a team composed of members of the internal audit department and of outside consultants to develop guidelines from which the standards could then be prepared. The scope of the effort was extended to include not only systems development but also computing centers, data bases, and the applications systems themselves.

Method

The team set the following objectives for the control standards:

1. Provide a framework within which the systems development and quality assurance groups can work when designing new systems.

2. Provide the internal audit department with a basis for review of new systems to ensure that adequate application controls are incorporated to prevent undetected errors and omissions and to provide suitable levels of protection against intentional acts.

3. Provide the internal audit department with a basis for review of EDP operations to ensure that adequate general controls are incorporated to prevent undetected errors and omissions and to provide suitable levels of protection against intentional acts.

The bank's internal audit department was responsible for developing the standards and thus made the major contributions. The consultant was assigned to assist internal audit and it refined the product, but "ownership" clearly lay with the bank.

The guidelines for the standards were submitted for review to various concerned groups. Chief among these were systems development, development support, quality assurance, and EDP operations. The reviewers were to determine whether the standards were technically feasible and pragmatic. When necessary, revisions were made to secure the agreement of all groups. When no agreement could be reached, the disputed point was referred to the level of management that spanned the disagreeing parties.

The project specified follow-up review to evaluate the effectiveness of the standards after several months of use.

Results

The project ran quite smoothly. The assignment of responsibilities for preparation and for review worked out well. The auditors established closer contact with the EDP professionals and both parties learned from the association. The mechanism for settling disagreements had to be used in only a few cases; peer review and informal methods effectively handled most problems. The post-implementation review resulted in worthwhile modifications of the standards.

Control Standards—Transaction Entry Phase, Applications Controls

Objective: To ensure that data entered into each application are complete, valid, and accurate and that data conversion is achieved fully and accurately.

Transaction Data Entry Controls

1. Each application should have written procedures covering transaction entry, highlighting system control points for the verification of data.
2. Each application should have adequate written user procedures covering input controls, input methods, and input schedules.
3. Wherever possible, input documents should be presented in a machine-readable form. Pre-encoding should be used wherever direct input is not feasible.
4. Remote data entry devices (e.g., terminals) should advise that all data has been sent. Automatic cut-off times may substitute when such advice is not received.

Proof and Balancing Controls

1. All value input should be subject to proof and balancing controls, with full verification and/or validity checking of value totals, batch totals, account numbers, and any sensitive data before transmission to/acceptance by computer. Use should be made of transmittal documents, containing all necessary control fields, wherever possible.
2. All nonvalue or maintenance input should be subject to document count and validity checking control to ensure completeness and validity of input before transmission to/acceptance by computer. Use should be made of transmittal documents, containing all necessary control fields, wherever possible.
3. All transactions processed through each application should receive a unique transaction identification (see Transaction Origination Controls).
4. All input should be subject to inbuilt edit routines to assist the accuracy and validity of capture. All reentered data should be subject to the same edit routines as original input.
5. Each application should provide for the manual verification of all essential control fields before release to computer processing.
6. Each application should provide for reports to input areas of values captured or for direct incorporation of data entry values into input area ledgers.

Terminal Entry Controls

1. To reduce the possibility of operator error, each application should provide for the optimum level of operator assistance.

    a. Standard format for data presentation and entry

    b. Optional computer-generated instructions, where possible

    c. Default values for nonessential fields

    d. Clearly identified error messages

    e. Minimization of fixed data input, with maximization of validation on variable data

    f. Response of fixed data (e.g., name) to enable validation before input of variable data).

2. There should be an adequate method of ensuring that any specified data can only be accessed by authorized persons via authorized terminals.

3. Where intelligent terminals are available, data should be subject to edit and validation procedures before transmission.

4. Application should provide for detection and warning to a secure hard-copy terminal for prompt review by, and regular report to, Operations management or Security Officer:

    a. All attempts to use a device not recognized by the system

    b. After an appropriate number of attempts to override password controls

    c. After an appropriate number of attempts to access restricted data

    d. After an appropriate number of attempts to input data unsuccessfully.

5. Application should provide for terminal access security by:

    a. Automatic log-off after an appropriate period of inactivity

    b. Automatic obliteration or nondisplay of passwords, wherever possible

    c. Provision of supervisor intervention for initiation and termination of terminal activity for each application.

6. There should be clear procedures established for the secure operation of data entry terminals, and all terminals should be subject to adequate levels of physical security at all times.

7. Each terminal should be identified as to authority levels, alterations to which may only be made by the Security Officer.

8. As far as possible, staff responsible for transaction entry should not be responsible for transaction origination or computer processing.

Error Controls

1. Each application should have written procedures covering all error types, the respective error handling procedures, methods of reentry, and the user's responsibility.

2. Error messages during input should be in standard format and terminology and should be unable to be overridden by users.

3. Errors not reentered before update is completed should be held in a separate suspense file and reported immediately (particularly value input).

Conclusions

The guidelines and resultant standards were structured to be as general as possible. This feature allowed freedom of choice to the developers and preserved the independence of the internal auditors.

All parties affected by the standards had the opportunity and responsibility of reviewing them. This was both technically and psychologically important: those who had to live by the standards had the chance to establish them, and the fact that each agency was made to feel that its opinion and insight were important contributed significantly to acceptance of the standards.

Part way through the project it became apparent that procedures for using the standards should be developed along with the standards themselves. Combining the development of standards with procedures for their use added significantly to their effectiveness and ease of applications. The accompanying example of transaction entry control standards is taken from the standards developed in this effort. It covers the transaction entry phase of application controls only. □

A Do-It-Yourself Project on Control Standards

1. Does your enterprise have an explicitly stated set of organization-wide control standards? If so, obtain it; if not, do standards exist in hidden form in certain policies, procedures, and memos? If so, assemble these and extract their essence.

2. How do the standards (formal or informal) that you have found compare with the suggestions for content found in the section "Content and Nature of Standards"? Arrange your standards to match the categories in that section. List the gaps and insufficiencies in coverage. What are the likely consequences of these shortfalls to your loss control program and to your organization's risk of loss?

3. Which organization elements and individuals have a direct stake in the development and promulgation of control standards in your organization? How can you best enlist their cooperation and support for your loss control program? Do they have any special interests that you can appeal to? Plan an education campaign to catch their attention and increase their knowledge.

4. What is the best way to organize to develop the standards? Who are the ideal team members? What are the best sources of outside help? Who should be the reviewers? What kind of schedule can be established for the development of the standards? What is the approximate budget for the task? Where should you take your proposal in order to get support and approval to proceed?

5. What will be the benefits of developing and installing the standards? How will the existence and enforcement of these standards change business processes in the enterprise?

A Perspective on Chapter 6

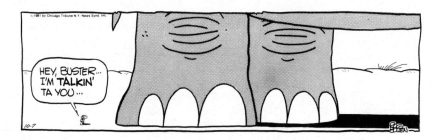

There is no constructiveness in this communication. Furthermore, it is all one-way—there is no "inter" in this action. (From "Animal Crackers," by Roger Bollen. Reprinted by permission of Tribune Company Syndicate, Inc.)

6

Foster Constructive Interaction

Management cannot simply decree a loss control program and then sit back and watch from the sidelines. It has a vital role as facilitator of action and communication among members of the loss control team. The principles of constructive interaction presented here are useful both in general and in the specific context of loss control.

Constructive interaction in EDP loss control is necessary for several practical reasons. First, the lessons learned and the subsequent sharing of that learning will lead to operational improvements. Things will run better and more reliably when users understand and appreciate the application of controls. The feedback effect of this better understanding will increase control effectiveness. Experience shows that people function better when their management and peers take the time to communicate constructively with them, explaining why and how the processes they are asked to perform are necessary and appropriate. This response is due partly to the attention paid by management and partly to better morale.

Constructive interaction provides direct savings in loss control in two ways: through reduction and avoidance of costs and through deterrence of intentional acts. When more people understand and are expected to participate in and contribute to the loss control objectives of the enterprise, ideas and initiatives tend to flow more freely and innovativeness grows. Constructive interaction results in ways to reduce and avoid costs by deterring, preventing, detecting, limiting, or correcting loss-causing acts. ■ A bank that initiated semiannual meetings of its EDP audit staff found many useful ideas coming out of each session. Also, when loss control is the topic of interaction among people who have access to assets, potential intentional acts against those assets are deterred, simply because interest in those assets and expectations of employee performance are made clear in one more way. Interviews with computer criminals disclose that the perpetrator often tries to excuse his or her act by saying, "Nobody told me not to do it" or "I didn't know it was wrong."

The most subtle, and in the long run most important, benefit of constructive interaction was put most succinctly by Oliver Wendell Holmes: "Man's mind, stretched by a new idea, will never return to its original dimension." Interacting with associates and subordinates or fostering other interaction among them stretches minds to broader dimensions and benefits both the individuals involved and the organization. One of the big challenges in EDP loss control is being comprehensive in considering assets, threats, controls, and vulnerabilities, because EDP is such a complex discipline. Constructive interaction helps ensure a comprehensive approach.

What Is Constructive Interaction?

Understanding the principles of constructive interaction requires a definition of its four components: interaction, constructiveness, interactors, and subject matter.

Interaction: It takes two (or more) to interact yet this simple fact is often forgotten. Think about the conversations you have observed (or been a party to) in which one person talked and the other sat with glazed eyeballs, clearly thinking about something else and ignoring the speaker, his voice, and most important, his ideas. The cartoon at the beginning of this chapter is an other example. So is junk mail; unless it is opened, read, and attended to, it is not communication.

Second, interaction requires a sense of parity or equality among the interactors. This does not mean that only peers can interact; far from it. Think about the last time you and your boss interacted about your salary. Rather, parity is conferred by some common understandings and some confluence of purpose among the interactors: "This is our problem; let's work on it together."

Next, interaction should be substantive; that is, it should be direct and to the point, to exclude the trivia that can obstruct the exchange of ideas. Substantiveness depends largely on structure and organization in the interaction process; the presence of these almost guarantees that good interaction is taking place.

Finally, interaction can take place through various media, sometimes two or three at a time. The medium most often involved in a loss control program is the printed page, but structured and unstructured people-to-people contact is also important. The media represent tools that can be used creatively to support the interaction. ■ The EDP department at one large savings and loan association set up a weekly meeting with an open agenda to discuss loss control problems and worked with the EDP auditors to circulate appropriate articles and papers in advance to stimulate discussion.

Constructiveness: Expert communicators believe that to be constructive, interaction must be germane, fair, nonthreatening, and unequivocal. Managers, and communicators in general, seem to know innately that these are good tests of constructiveness, but they often find it hard to apply them to their own dealings with other people.

The first criterion, that the interaction be germane, seems almost trivial in one sense. "Everybody knows" what the subject of the interaction is. However, the interaction can be pertinent in the mind of one person but not in that of the other. The personal context within which each party understands the interaction may be similar, but they are almost never identical. ■ Consider a meeting to discuss controls in an application system under development. The developer and the auditor start from quite different vantage points and with different objectives in mind. The first step toward effective communication is to exchange some understanding of viewpoints so that the communication can be germane to both. The most important of these is, "This topic is important to me because . . . ." Taking the time to tell others why you want their attention ensures that the first criterion of constructiveness is met. ■ In responding to criticism from the external auditor concerning inadequate control of activities and access privileges of systems programmers in their company, the manager of systems programming and the internal EDP auditor were able to carry on a constructive dialogue after each had listened carefully and sympathetically to the other's viewpoint and interpretation of responsiblities.

For interaction to be fair, it must embody not only the element of parity discussed above but also fairness in structure and content. Fairness in structure implies that all parties to the interaction can contribute or object to the process and feel sure that the input will be received on its merits. Fairness in content is closely related: the interaction should deal with facts whenever possible, and when that is not possible, perceptions and speculations should be clearly labeled as such.

Constructive interaction is nonthreatening. Deal with "touchy" topics in the context of facts, not of emotions, and address corrective, not punitive, actions: "What can we learn from this experience?" The destructive potential of an interaction that sounds threatening is substantial and long-lived.

Finally, to be constructive, interaction must be unequivocal. Some memos, sometimes even whole reports, leave the reader wondering, "What did he or she say?" Writing more clearly and avoiding jargon is an important part of meeting this criterion, but clear thinking must precede both. Answering several questions beforehand can help: "What do I want to achieve by this interaction?" "How can I avoid the wrong result?" "What can I do to make my interlocuter play back to me some signs that he understands?" The

---

Good Intentions, Bad Results

In 1980 one of the authors was acting as a consultant to the president of a $500 million food products division of a major conglomerate, seeking ways to improve the effectiveness of its EDP department. The company had pressed very hard to grow fast and to provide some innovative EDP systems to support that growth. For many reasons, the systems development activities had not gone smoothly. The president was a brilliant, dedicated executive who wanted the best for his company and was prepared to fight for it. He gave personal attention to the problems with systems development and interviewed managers and technicians to try to find out where the problems were and to identify and secure the resources necessary to solve the problems. Because his intervention seemed to have no effect, or sometimes even a negative effect, he turned to a consultant for help. Investigation revealed many latent problems and in some areas lack of candor in discussing them with the president.

The president's interactions with the systems people were part of the problem. He asked incisive questions that often dealt with detail. The overall impression these questions created was a threatening one. Although the president was trying to be constructive, the combination of his position, intellect, and persistence made his interlocutors defensive and anxious to smooth over potential problems in order to get off the hot seat.

---

last question is perhaps the best tool in avoiding equivocation. Hearing one's ideas played back, with or without agreement, is the final test of unequivocal interaction.

The interactors: Those involved in the loss control process form two groups: those who have direct control of assets and those who have indirect control. The first group generally includes workers such as a clerk in the payroll or accounts payable department or a data control clerk in EDP who knows the combination to the safe containing the signature plates for the check-signing machine. Those with indirect control are generally managers: the head of payroll, the treasurer of the company, the manager of EDP systems development whose system designers ensure that proper controls are included in the new inventory system. Thus there can be three pairings of interactors: worker with worker, manager with manager, and manager with worker.

Managers concerned about EDP loss control want the people in direct control of assets to interact with one another about loss control. The latter have the detailed skills, knowledge, and access that can preserve or threaten those assets. Sharing their knowledge and experience with their peers constructively can improve control over EDP-related losses.

Managers must communicate with managers also to share knowledge and experience, but they have other responsibilites too. Two important parts of the manager's job are planning and measuring. In the context of EDP loss control, these functions demand constructive interaction among managers to support the planning process for the deterrence, prevention, detection, limiting, and correction of EDP losses. ■ Several companies accomplish this through a loss control advisory committee or similar group consisting of key managers concerned with the problem. Similarly, managers must organize and execute effective, integrated measurement of EDP loss prevention activities and losses.

Finally, managers must interact with workers to explain objectives, strategies, plans, and programs; and workers must feed back results (or lack of them) and ideas to managers for improving the loss control program.

Subject matter: Constructive interaction involves four kinds of subject matter: facts, directions, ideas, and solicitations.

Facts are statements that are verifiable in the real world. But how does one handle situations that are not directly verifiable? The solution is to make a factual statement about the uncertainty or to burrow through imprecise ideas to underlying facts. Compare "A lot of computer crime goes unreported" with "We have seven instances from our research in which the injured party decided not to prosecute because of potential embarrassment." Directions are instructions to someone to do something. Generally they allow some latitude, and some are accompanied by facts to explain or edify, but basically they are structured to make something happen. Directions must meet the tests of constructiveness, and their author must remember that interaction is involved. Ideas are not facts; they cannot yet be verified. They are communicated to stimulate thinking, bolster arguments, and categorize or order facts. They too must meet the tests of constructiveness. Most difficult to handle as subject matter are solicitations. In this context, solicitations are door-openers, opportunities for others to communicate with you. The forbidding president described above did not know how to use solicitations as elements in interaction. Solicitations are, in essence, interested questions directed to an interlocutor that ask for thoughts, innovations, feelings, and the like. They always use and emphasize the word *you*: "What do *you* think?" "How would *you* do it?"

How Can You Foster Constructive Interaction?

When someone wants to change another person's behavior, there seem to be only two lasting and humane ways to do it: by making it easier to behave in the desired way or by establishing incentives for the desired behavior. Both approaches are useful in the control of EDP-related losses through constructive interaction.

Improving understanding makes it easier to behave in the desired way. The three major avenues are education, on-the-job training, and cross-disciplinary experience. It is sometimes easy to forget that the majority of people concerned with the deterrence, prevention, detection, limiting, and correction of EDP-related losses are unlikely to have had much formal education on the subject. Until very recently, colleges offered no regular courses on these matters. Today, seminars and books devote more attention to the subject, but the average EDP systems designer, for example, probably has no academic background in the selection and implementation of financial controls in the EDP systems he or she is hired to design. Academic training, discussed in detail in chapter 7, provides technical grounding in loss control that will make it easier for managers and workers to interact constructively. For much the same reasons, on-the-job training complements academic experience in helping foster constructive interaction.

The most valuable tool in promoting constructive interaction is cross-disciplinary experience. EDP loss control calls upon many disciplines, including systems design, programming, accounting, auditing, line management, and data security administration. No one discipline can do it all. Temporarily taking on the duties of others involved in the control effort will help each member of the team develop appreciation of the needs and problems of other members. Most Japanese companies, and some U.S. companies in their management training programs, deliberately rotate at least some people through several jobs. This approach has special value in EDP loss control. ■ One major oil company has established a policy that any aspirant to management advancement in the company has to serve a tour of duty in the internal audit department. The rationale is simple: the candidate gets a special and revealing view of the company's activities and at the same time becomes very aware of the need for effective loss control.

In addition to these measures, it is useful and desirable to provide incentives. The simplest incentive—and one of the cheapest—is a show of interest by management, chiefly through the creation, implementation, and continued support of the loss control program. The existence and easy availability of effective channels of communication to upper levels of management also serves to convince employees that loss control is important. An effective loss reporting system is one such channel. A straightforward, no-nonsense attitude about loss control also fosters constructiveness. ■ A major computer manufacturer issues time-sharing passwords to its employees in their paycheck envelopes, a convincing demonstration of managerial interest in the value and sanctity of the password.

Finally, management can foster constructive interaction by rewarding behavior. It can seek out and publicize successes, reward their authors, and strongly suggest that others imitate the successful methods. Doing these things requires a continuous and strong evaluative element and mechanisms to disseminate information throughout the organization.

There are several ways of spreading information about loss control. Seminars, both external and in-house, are effective. EDP systems reviews that focus on loss control aspects can often be set up as part of the regular systems development process. Periodicals and books can be circulated and a loss control library maintained. Regularly scheduled and scrupulously attended external or in-house meetings can be powerful vehicles for marshaling opinion and motivation and for exchanging worthwhile ideas. All of these activities are most valuable if they are multidisciplinary.

CASE STUDY

Background

☐ The internal audit branch of a large federal agency hired a consulting firm to teach it new techniques in EDP audit and security and to map out a program for increasing its skills and operations in EDP loss control. The internal audit organization had a reputation for quality work in operational audits and substantial success in finding opportunities for improvements. At the beginning of the project the department was weak in the disciplines of EDP audit and had only a small staff of EDP auditors, all dedicated to developing EDP-oriented audit tools to be used by the rest of the staff to speed up traditional audits. Management of the agency was sympathetic to the consulting project and open-minded about possible results.

Method

The client requested four specific activities: (1) a two-week seminar on the general subject of EDP loss control for its auditors; (2) on-the-job training of the same auditors, in the form of EDP loss control reviews of two of the agency's major operations; (3) preparation of an EDP loss control guideline for the agency; and (4) a long-range plan for the EDP audit organization.

The seminar was divided into two sessions, one on the East Coast and one on the West. The first review occurred between the sessions to provide time for fine-tuning the content of the seminar to the interests and experience of the audience. The consultants had based the seminar on a series used many times in public presentations in the United States and around the world; thus they confidently expected a routine activity.

The first seminar was attended by about fifteen working auditors, most of whom had only a little understanding of EDP processes. The initial presentations therefore included a lot of grounding in EDP technology. The group paid close attention to descriptions of the problems of computer abuse and to the basic fundamentals of risk analysis, but as the seminar entered the discussion of EDP audit techniques and the like, impatience and skepticism began to surface. The consultants did not at the time understand the cause, but it was clear that communications with students were not effective.

A few weeks later, most of the seminar group traveled with one of the consultants to an agency installation in another city. There the group conducted a two-week EDP loss control review of the agency's payroll function. Each auditor was assigned to one of several two-person teams who reviewed, under consultant direction, various aspects of the operation. They then prepared and presented to the local agency executive the comments, conclusions, and recommendations. During this time the consultants and the clients got to know one another much better, became more frank in their interactions, and the source and nature of the problems that had surfaced in the first session of the seminar became clearer.

The auditors' frustration with the methods that had been shown them was twofold. First, they were too "theoretical"—a word which translated into "These approaches require a commitment of time on my part to learn and to use, and my boss pushes too hard for audit results to allow me to use these methods." Second, the auditors thought that performance in their organization was to be measured by the number of unfavorable findings they made in each audit—the more such findings, the better the next performance review.

Production of the EDP loss control guide proceeded smoothly, with many useful contributions from the internal audit branch. The contributions were specific and aimed at finding easily documentable deficiencies; thus, all reflected a desire to meet the presumed criterion for success in auditing.

Discussions with internal audit management did not bear out the perceptions of the auditors at the working level. The consultants found executives genuinely interested in effecting improvements in the organizations they audited, and they clearly did not measure their success by counting the number of unfavorable findings.

Results

The consultants compared the executive and auditor interview results with the agency's promotion history and found little to justify the auditors' feelings. They did find, however, that the auditors traveled a lot and were out of touch with their management most of the time. There was an active informal peer network but no regular communication between management and individual auditors. The training courses were the agency's only recent attempt to build the skills of the internal audit group. This lack of training had led to a general feeling that they were being "squeezed" through overwork to build a reputation for the organization at the expense of the individuals. Their response was to slant their audits to uncover errors that would get them attention and subsequent reward.

The consultants replanned the remaining seminar and the on-site EDP loss control review. They included presentations from upper levels of agency management explaining their viewpoint on the audit activities and objectives of the organization. They also concentrated on case studies and problem solving as vehicles for teaching the subject matter. During the on-site EDP loss control review that followed, more time was devoted to fewer activities, giving the on-the-job trainees a better chance to understand how they could apply the methods to do a better, more effective and expeditious audit.

The long-range plan prepared for the audit organization included three tangible recommendations: (1) a careful buildup of investment in education and training for the staff, (2) institution of a newsletter to keep the staff better informed of EDP loss control activities and developments, and (3) expansion of a cross-training program that trained auditors in EDP disciplines and brought a limited number of EDP professionals onto the audit staff as consultants. Finally, the consultants counseled the executives of the internal audit organization about the misconceptions held by the audit staff and suggested periodic conclaves of both executives and audit staff to improve interaction among all levels.

Conclusions

This case emphasizes the communications pitfalls that can develop in an organization of mobile, independently working people. The goals and objectives may be clear to management, and current staff activities may appear to serve these objectives, but feedback is necessary to communicate to everyone how management evaluates staff performance. □

An Experiment in Fostering Constructive Interaction

1. Examine your own organization and compile a list of areas that would benefit from better communications about EDP loss control. List the benefits and assign a value to them. Categorize them as tangible and intangible and try to quantify as many of the intangibles as possible.
2. List and evaluate the present interaction processes concerning loss control in your company. Categorize them by who the interactors are and what the subject matter is. Do they meet the tests of constructiveness?
3. Take roughly 25 percent of the total benefits obtained in step 1 and treat it as a budget to spend on various approaches to improving interaction about EDP loss control in your company. What are your priorities? Which interactors are involved?
4. Develop an approach to measure the effect of the actions you propose. How can the realization of the benefits be proved?
5. Put all of these into a proposal and send it to your boss for approval.

A Perspective on Chapter 7

Ideas about auditing, especially vigorous auditing, seem to be conditioned by images like this one. It is time to change these ideas radically. (From "Broom-Hilda," by Russell Myers. Reprinted by permission of Tribune Company Syndicate, Inc.)

7

Support a Vigorous EDP Audit Organization

The auditor plays an important role in EDP loss control, and that role is not just an after-the-fact one of review. This chapter discusses three characteristics that make an EDP audit organization vigorous and effective in EDP loss control. They are:

- Independence
- Competence
- A long-range plan

The focus of this chapter is EDP auditors, a special group within internal audit. Because their primary role is that of auditors, these characteristics are applicable to the audit organization as a whole.

Independence

Independence is essential to the proper and useful functioning of an internal audit organization. In well-run enterprises, internal audit is the one department that is independent in both form and substance and thus can provide valuable information on compliance reviews and evaluations. The basic health of the enterprise depends on the allocation of sufficient resources and expertise to keep this department free to address all important areas. This principle is crucial to maintaining a vigorous EDP audit function.

In addition to this basic justification for independence, there is a second reason: a considerable body of opinion makes a vigorous audit organization almost a legal requirement. For example, the Foreign Corrupt Practices Act did not explicitly mandate internal audit departments, but in talking about the act, Harold M. Williams, then chairman of the SEC, said, "One factor to be considered by companies seeking assurance that they are in compliance with the FCPA . . . is effective use of their internal audit staffs."

A third rationale derives from experience: an audit department that is strong and functioning well does help reduce losses; controls are stronger, and management is better informed.

The need for audit independence is well established within the audit profession, but it has not always been clear how to foster that independence. Following are a number of ways in which independence of the EDP audit function can be developed and strengthened.

Strong mandate: EDP audit should have a strong, formal mandate defined in its charter or its statement of responsibility. This mandate should be written, formalized, and should clearly define scope, responsibility, and authority. ■ As a reflection of the fundamental importance of this mandate, one organization includes its full audit charter on the inside of its standard audit report cover.

The mandate should be broad enough to include all aspects of the EDP environment—hardware, facilities, software (both systems and applications), and people. The mandate should also include any decentralized or distributed EDP environments in the organization. The audit function exists to serve management. The best way to facilitate this service (assuming expertise and resources are available) is to give auditors wide latitude and the requisite authority.

The accompanying examples contain parts of EDP audit mandates from two organizations in different parts of the country.

Audit freedom: The EDP audit function should be able to perform audits in any area within its scope (as defined in the mandate). The timing should be at the discretion of the audit department. The freedom to choose area and timing must be tempered by good judgment and business considerations. Performing surprise audits poses a difficulty. The occasional need for fast, unannounced audits must be balanced against constructive performance and development of a positive rapport with all areas of the organization. Our experience indicates that surprise audits should be within the charter of the audit function but should be executed with extreme care and with well-defined justification, such as when there is strong suspicion and preliminary evidence of illegal acts or when directed by regulatory agencies.

EDP Audit Section Charter of a Large Midwestern Bank

Purpose

The purpose of the EDP Audit Section is to review activities throughout the bank but primarily in the Computer Department which involve computer software and hardware. The primary focus of these reviews is to evaluate internal control over systems (both automated and manual) and computer hardware. The section also provides substantial support to the Financial Audit Sections in the maintenance of the audit software packages which belong to the Auditing Division.

Authority

The EDP Audit Section has full authority to review anything at any time as deemed appropriate by the Section Manager in discharging the section's responsibilities. This authority is absolute and is necessary to maintain audit independence.

In addition, the EDP Audit Section has full authority to discharge its responsibilities in compliance with the *Standards for the Professional Practice of Internal Auditing*, published by the Institute of Internal Auditors.

EDP Audit Charter of a Large Southern Savings and Loan Association

Purpose

The purpose of the EDP Audit Section is to review EDP-related activities throughout the Association. The primary focus of these reviews is to evaluate the system of internal controls (both manual and automated), the effectiveness of EDP operations, and the integrity of the data.

Scope

The EDP Audit Section shall have unrestricted access to all EDP-related procedures, operations, records, facilities, and personnel of the Association. This includes: computerized application systems from the origination of transactions through processing and delivery of output; development and modification of hardware and software systems; and computer hardware and facilities. The scope covers the main computer operations and all decentralized or distributed configurations in the Association and its wholly owned subsidiaries.

Top-level access: EDP audit should have direct access to the top management of the organization and to the audit committee of the board of directors or to the board chairman if there is no audit committee. This access can be established formally by a direct reporting line to the audit committee. Informal access is developed by building mutual trust and credibility between audit and senior management.

To provide administrative support the audit function can have a "dotted line" reporting relationship to some business department such as the controller's office, treasury, finance, or accounting. The key factor for success is a clear understanding that responsibility goes directly to the board and that any disputes will be handled there. ■ The head auditor of a West Coast leasing firm makes it a habit to forward to members of the board of directors news items and short journal articles dealing with computer losses and loss control.

Open relationship with external auditors: The audit department should have and support a continuing, open relationship with the organization's external auditing firm and any regulatory bodies that are mandated to perform examinations. This relationship should result in a positive formal and informal flow of information, which can guide internal audit in planning and developing priorities for areas that need audits.

Access to outside consultants: The audit department should have access to consultants and budgetary resources to use them when needed. Consultants may be needed to help review a very technical area, support the staff in a special audit, produce an audit tool such as an audit program, or provide training. The benefits of using consultants are twofold. First, consultants bring real professional expertise to the solution of problems. Second, because consultants are outsiders and experts (that is, they come from more than fifty miles away), their findings and recommendations often carry more weight and are more likely to be accepted by management.

Breadth of access: The audit function should have open and immediate access to all departments and staff. As with choosing areas to audit, discretion should be used so as not to disrupt business unnecessarily. Constructive auditing demands timely and informed analysis and reporting. These are possible only when auditors have full access to all parts of an organization.

Resources to support independence: A number of tangible resources can help strengthen and maintain audit independence: control objectives, standards, and guidelines; computer access; a library of relevant books, journals, and articles; and access to special support from other functions.

The Authority of a Consultant

Consultants were retained to make a brief review of EDP security and control in an organization in which development of applications was centralized and processing was distributed among several centers around the country. The review identified areas needing further, in-depth investigation. At the very beginning of the project the client liaison, who was not a security expert but a good manager/analyst, identified several areas that he knew were weak. One of these was the lack of a library package to regulate the computer program change control process and distribution to the field. He said that it had not been corrected because the head of the organization (a very qualified individual) had so dictated.

When the review identified areas requiring more analysis, the client asked the consultants to list the recommendations that they felt should be acted upon at once and those that could be made without further analysis. One recommendation was to get a commercially available library package. In the final debriefing, the head of the organization listened, asked questions, and gave instructions to his staff. On hearing the recommendation regarding the library package, he turned and asked the project liaison, "Why don't we have a package?" After some brief discussions among the staff, the order was given to take action that week on getting a package. After the meeting the liaison manager expressed satisfaction: he could now get a package to reduce a vulnerability, the organization would be better controlled, and no one had had his or her ego crushed or blood pressure inflated.

Control objectives, standards, and guidelines. The organization and the audit department itself are strengthened by the development and use of control objectives, standards, and guidelines. Audit should develop the control objectives and review the standards and guidelines, as discussed in chapter 5.

Computer access. At the minimum, internal audit should have accounts to allow use of the computer system and any necessary accompanying resources such as terminals, documentation, and training. Auditors need to have access to the computer system for four purposes: (1) to access data for confirmations and to assist external auditors in their attest function; (2) to review programs for their integrity and conformance to standards; (3) to use the resource regularly for planning, bookkeeping, data reduction, and automated (programmed) analysis of data and programs; and (4) to exercise or test the system in general to determine if it works as claimed. We strongly discourage efforts to break, crash, or penetrate the system without at least the knowledge of the data processing function. Such efforts can create significant technical problems and can also create adversary relationships between the audit and other departments. These developments will compromise the credibility and constructiveness of the audit function.

Using the in-house computer system also has a positive psychological effect. Auditors who experience problems and frustrations in getting their work done—often while coping with controls that they may have recommended—are likely to temper their findings and recommendations with pragmatism. Also, the credibility of auditors should increase as data processing people become aware that they are using the system.

Except in the research and academic communities, the concept of the audit department's having its own computer has had limited application. Auditors often express their need for an independent audit computer with the rationale, "If I'm supposed to be looking for unauthorized modifications to programs, modifications made by data processing people, how can I do it if I have to use data processing's computer? They can cover their tracks without my knowing." This overstatement of the case does have a legitimate basis: the computer peripheral devices and the operation of the resource are usually totally controlled by data processing people. It is technically possible for someone in data processing (say, a systems programmer) to make unauthorized changes to the software that will cover tracks when audit makes requests for data such as listings of programs. Currently, however, the compensating controls available are more cost effective in reducing the risk than supplying EDP audit with its own computer would be.

Some organizations apply a compromise approach and use a commercially available time-sharing service. Key data bases (such as "sanitized" copies of the payroll and accounts payable files) can be stored there for comparison with currently used versions. Data processing (such as selection of records for confirmations) can also be done on a limited basis.

Library. There is a significant amount of useful literature about the EDP audit function and it should be made easily available to auditors for reference. The number of books, journals, and articles produced on the topic in the last five to ten years fully justifies a library. Because the profession is still in its infancy, the learning curve is very steep and each new idea, approach, or case study adds significantly to the information on the subject. Also, because the computer field tends to be technically oriented, EDP auditors need guidance on different specific technical areas. The annotated bibliography at the back of this book lists the major items that would be appropriate in an EDP audit library.

Special support from other functions. EDP auditors are expected to have a high level of technical knowledge. However, they cannot be expected to be experts in all the areas they may have to review. EDP auditors should be able to call on technical experts in the organization to provide a short period of consultation with a narrow scope within the overall review. The expert will help educate the auditor; evaluate ideas, findings, and recommendations already prepared by the auditor; respond to specific audit questions (for example "What are the major exposures, controls, and vulnerabilities in this area?"); and give professional advice for any pertinent topic not already considered. Primary areas that may require special support include data communications and networks, data base management systems, operating systems (and other system software), environmental support systems (such as power supply and air conditioning), building architecture, and distributed data processing. Auditors can be expected to develop expertise in areas that are important for their organization, but they will sometimes still need outside support. ■ The manager of EDP audit for a large manufacturing organization understood that his department lacked expertise in dealing with the operating system and functions performed by systems programmers. He retained experts from the organization's external audit firm to work with them in reviewing the area.

Some argue that calling on special support from inside the organization can compromise audit independence. However, the resultant credibility and constructive service to the organization far outweigh the risk, as long as support is called on only when clearly required and the auditor takes full responsibility for the final audit report.

Competence

A second critical component in developing a vigorous EDP audit organization, and one that parallels independence, is competence. Competence provides quality, value, and credibility in the audit process and in its results. Today the demand for EDP auditors far exceeds the supply, and the trends of technology and of business both indicate that this demand will continue in the next few years. Therefore, the training and education of EDP auditors is a critical aspect of developing a vigorous EDP audit organization. The profession is new, there are constant changes in the field of computer science that require additional knowledge, and few auditors have the necessary level of training and education. However, organizations do not always support this need. A survey by the Institute of Internal Auditors (IIA), published in *Sys-*

Tools for Developing and Strengthening Independence

1. Strong mandate
2. Audit freedom
3. Top-level access
4. Open relationship with external auditors
5. Access to outside consultants
6. Breadth of access
7. Resources

---

tems Auditability and Control in 1977, indicated that of the organizations responding, 50 percent had no training and education budget for EDP audit, 45 percent had a training and education budget allocation amounting to less than 5 percent of the EDP audit budget (that is, less than 5 percent of available staff hours and related costs), and only 5 percent allocated more than 5 percent of the EDP audit budget for training and education. We believe that a minimum of 5 to 7 percent of the total audit budget should be spent on training and education for each staff member. This translates into two to three weeks of training and education plus the associated costs of travel, tuition, and documents. Admittedly this amount of time is often hard to allocate, but it should be considered a highly desirable goal for the vigorous EDP audit organization.

The same study analyzed the main training and education areas needed to perform competent EDP auditing and identified the following as basic topics of education, appropriate for auditors having little or no EDP education or experience:

- Introduction to EDP
- Computer hardware overview
- Computer programming overview
- Computer documentation overview
- Introduction to EDP application controls
- Introduction to general EDP controls

More specialized or advanced areas, intended for experienced EDP auditors, include:

- On-line systems controls
- Data communication controls
- Continuous operation controls
- Storage media/device controls
- Audit trace considerations
- Special audit software
- Case studies

In addition to its value in the development of staff expertise, a training and education program provides incentives for recruiting and keeping staff and for providing career path opportunities in the organization for individuals who lack extensive technical knowledge of EDP. Two examples accompanying this section present the program for EDP audit staff training and education established by one major transportation firm.

EDP Audit Staff Training Program

Purpose

Directly develop in-house personnel in their EDP auditing skills.

Method

Establish levels of EDP auditors (e.g., Senior EDP Audit Specialist, EDP Audit Specialist, and EDP Audit Trainee). Set knowledge and training standards for each level. Determine individual's training needs. Provide training opportunities within the audit schedule.

Organization

Establish EDP Audit teams with various required levels of audit expertise. Staff outside of EDP Audit may be used as required. Determine the requirements of the team in relation to the type of audit activity. Prepare an audit plan tailored to the available staff. Train the staff to perform the audit function as needed.

On-the-Job Training

Have experienced EDP auditors work with less experienced staff so that the experience may be passed on, emphasizing planning, audit programs, use of EDP audit tools, working paper techniques, and reporting requirements.

In-House Training

In-house training offered by data processing, user departments, and internal audit should be attended by audit staff members when appropriate. Auditors with little EDP background or experience should make extensive use of these courses, while others should attend those that will directly increase their effectiveness in planned audit efforts.

EDP offers a variety of video-based courses designed for both introduction and advanced development. These courses are periodically available and should be used by EDP auditors when appropriate. User departments also offer training for their staff in the procedures and operations that support applications. EDP auditors should attend these sessions when they are addressing application areas that will be part of a planned audit. Internal Audit also offers courses and seminars appropriate for EDP auditors without strong audit background.

A Long-Range Plan

The third essential element in a vigorous EDP audit organization is a long-range plan. EDP audit should have formal planning, just like any other business function. The planning process for EDP audit should include all the

EDP Audit Staff Education Program

A staff education program for EDP auditors is desirable for professional development and for meeting the auditing needs of the company. The overall program is
designed to address the ongoing needs of both new and experienced EDP
auditors.

Education

All EDP Audit staff should have strong academic and professional education or
equivalent job experience. This stems from the need for professional knowledge,
analysis ability, and communication (oral and written) skills. This standard can be
measured by licensing in a professional society, obtaining a college degree, or
management's evaluation of job experience. The company supports these
efforts by allocating staff time and underwriting associated costs.

Specific courses (topic areas) in the EDP area that should be part of the formal
education program include:

- Introduction to data processing
- Hardware overview
- Systems analysis and programming (COBOL)
- Data processing documentation
- System software overview (operating systems and utilities)
- Data base management concepts
- Decentralized and distributed systems concepts
- Introduction to internal controls
- EDP controls
- Audit software
- EDP audit tools and techniques
- Minicomputer audit and control

These courses and others, if not part of a formal education, may be available
in-house or from community colleges, vendors (hardware and software), public

steps and reviews that apply to planning for other departments. Because
EDP audit is a relatively new field, there are additional strong reasons for
planning. These include the need to:

- Increase the interest and awareness of senior management.
- Provide a mechanism for management review and evaluation of the
  function.
- Define the direction of audit involvement.
- Reduce the chance of surprises and the counterproductive effort that
  usually accompanies surprises.

accounting firms, consulting firms, and professional associations such as the American Institute of Certified Public Accountants (AICPA), IIA, the Canadian Institute of Chartered Accountants (CICA), and the EDP Auditors Association.

Certification

All staff members are encouraged and will be appropriately supported to pursue certification. An EDP Audit manager should also have, or be actively working towards, certification in one or more of the certification programs. (Certified Internal Auditor, Certified Public Accountant, and Certified Information Systems Auditor).

Also, membership in the associated professional societies is encouraged. Time and support will be provided to allow for active participation.

Academic Achievement

All staff members are encouraged and will be appropriately supported to obtain an academic degree (a B.A. or B.S.). The areas of concentration include computer science, mathematics, accounting, or business. It is desirable for an EDP Audit manager also to have an advanced degree, specifically an MBA.

Continuing Education

As is required by the certification programs, there is a policy of continuing education. The company encourages continuing education and professional development such as multiday seminars, professional society meetings, vendor education courses, conferences, and self-study courses. The company supports these efforts to a level of two to four weeks per year.

Library

To support the staff education program, an EDP Audit library is maintained. Documents should include books, government publications, vendor literature, journal articles, self-study material, and periodicals.

- Provide guidance for training and education programs.
- Provide guidance for the allocation of resources—primarily staff.

The long-range plan is more than a simple schedule and thus should not be developed to meet an arbitrary time span but rather to meet the long-term needs of the organization. Ideally the plan should be formulated to mesh with organization-wide goals and objectives. If the organization does not have a long-range plan, the EDP audit plan could be used as a starting point to develop one.

The plan should consider assets, exposures, and audit objectives. Any asset that needs to be protected must have controls to protect it, and in turn these controls should be audited to ensure that they are adequate and operate properly. To the extent that management considers the protection of certain exposures important, EDP audit's long-range plan should address these. Finally, audit objectives and the specific audit tasks and programs that support the objectives should be applied to the assets and exposures to define specific action to protect and control the assets from loss due to the exposures.

CASE STUDY

Background

☐ A major transportation firm had long made effective use of traditional auditing. As its business grew and greatly diversified, it recognized the necessity to expand its capabilities in EDP auditing. To provide better focus for the activities of its EDP audit department, the firm started by developing an EDP audit long-range plan, using a team composed of both staff and consultants.

Method

The first step was to define elements to be used in the planning:

1. Assets included four major data centers, the major application systems in place, and major application systems being developed.
2. Exposures were an expansion of the nine basic ones cited in figure 3, namely, loss of management control, erroneous record keeping, unacceptable accounting, business interruptions, erroneous management decisions, fraud or embezzlement, statutory sanctions, excessive costs, deficient revenues, loss or destruction of assets, and competitive disadvantage.
3. Audit tasks were defined for production applications, data centers, and systems software and hardware.

The second step was to establish an exposures matrix, shown in figure 13, that correlated EDP audit tasks with areas of exposure. The resultant matrix indicates the audit tasks that address the exposures. After management had assigned a relative importance to each exposure, the matrix was analyzed and the various audit tasks that addressed managerial concerns were identified.

EDP Audit Function	Exposures										
	Management control	Erroneous recordkeeping	Unacceptable accounting	Business interruption	Erroneous management decisions	Fraud or embezzlement	Statutory sanctions	Excessive costs	Deficient revenues	Loss/destruction of assets	Competitive disadvantage
Production Applications											
Design & development		✓			✓			✓			
Post-implementation		✓	✓		✓		✓	✓	✓		✓
Program integrity		✓	✓		✓	✓	✓	✓	✓		
Distributed processing			✓	✓	✓	✓		✓	✓	✓	
On-line applications			✓			✓				✓	✓
Recovery				✓	✓	✓		✓		✓	
Data base management		✓						✓		✓	
Security							✓			✓	
User education	✓										
Data Centers											
Security				✓		✓		✓		✓	
Facilities				✓						✓	
Disaster recovery				✓						✓	
Off-site storage						✓				✓	
Operations		✓		✓	✓					✓	
Systems Software/Hardware											
Operating software				✓							
Systems libraries/files				✓							
Systems hardware				✓						✓	
Utility software				✓				✓		✓	
Time sharing (TSO)		✓				✓					
Remote job entry		✓				✓					
Vendor software						✓		✓			

Figure 13. *Exposures matrix*

The third step was to plan the general level of audit growth in the major audit areas—production applications, data centers, and system software and hardware. Figure 14 shows the growth plan based on the assignment of exposure priorities. For example, the data centers were considered important enough and involving enough exposures to warrant a yearly audit. To give the department enough time to reach this level, it was planned to perform one additional data center audit each year until all four were being audited

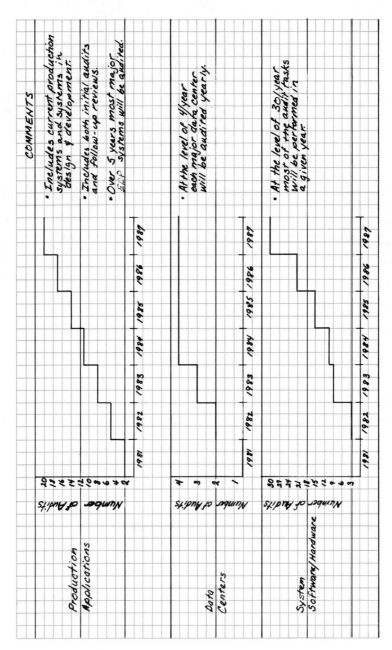

Figure 14.   *EDP audit growth plan*

annually. This time frame extended from the present to the time when the sufficient audits were being planned to meet the level of concern expressed by management.

The fourth step was to establish staff requirements for each audit task and then calculate the total staff requirements for the total implementation period. Figure 15 shows part of the final long-range plan. The level-of-effort projections were used in requesting and justifying additional staff.

Each row represents separate audit tasks in each of the three major areas. The columns represent the time frame for the plan. A bar in the matrix indicates that, for the corresponding audit task, the department will have the expertise to perform the task and that performing the task in the given time frame is *desired*. Values are given for the total estimated level of effort for each major area but not for specific tasks. (This would be included in short-term plans.)

Results

As with most plans, there was a fair amount of feedback and iteration before management reviewed and accepted this one. Since then, the company has used the plan as the basis for adding staff and scheduling audits. There has been some slippage in meeting the staffing levels, but this is the result of subsequently enlarging the time frame (defining fifteen-month "years"), not of eliminating areas to audit.

Conclusions

The company audit organization found the long-range plan to be a powerful tool in justifying its needs for more EDP audit staff and for more education and training funds. At a more subtle level, the existence of the plan has provided direction to the activities of the audit department and a sense of purpose to its staff. □

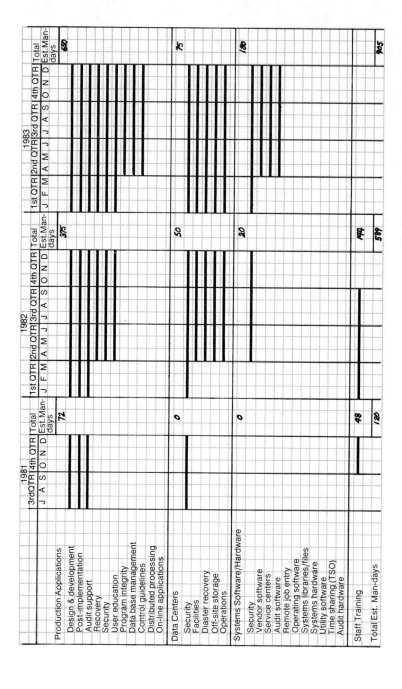

Figure 15. *Final long-range plan*

Assess the Climate for the EDP
Audit Function in Your Organization

1. Is there a written mandate for (EDP) audit? If so, obtain it. Does it provide enough latitude and authority? If not, is there an unwritten mandate? How widespread is knowledge of it? Are there any actions you should take to improve the situation?
2. What scope and authority does the audit program have?
3. Does your audit group have and use access to top-level management and the board of directors?
4. Does your audit group have an effective relationship with the external auditors?
5. When did the audit group last use outside consultants? When could outside consultants last have contributed materially to an audit?
6. Does the audit group have freedom of access to all parts of the organization?
7. List the resources available to the audit group. Does it have suitable access to computers? to a library of technical and professional literature? to experts in technical fields? Does it have well-documented control objectives, standards, and guidelines?
8. Does your organization have a training and professional development program for EDP auditors? How well supported is it by budget and management commitments?

A Perspective on Chapter 8

Many EDP professionals still believe that developing information systems is an art, or at best an inexact science. Such professionals behave accordingly, and the result is systems with inherent failures of many types, but especially failures of control. This chapter focuses on how positive participation by a broad range of concerned specialists and generalists in the systems development process can contribute to systems integrity. (From "Frank and Ernest," by Bob Thaves. Reprinted by permission. Copyright © 1980 NEA, Inc.)

8

Support Broad Participation in EDP Systems Development

Systems development is important for several reasons, but most of all because it is a fundamental business process. Every business depends on procedures to accomplish its operations. These procedures routinize and thereby simplify and facilitate operations. EDP systems development is simply an extension of the process of creating and implementing these procedures through the use of the powerful business tool called the computer.

EDP systems development is receiving more and more attention from management. Often the development of the EDP system to support a new product, to analyze data in a new way, or to present new decision support information to management is the limiting item in the growth of a business. Systems development is absorbing an increasing share of the dollars spent on information services in most companies; today it is not unusual to spend 0.5 to 1 percent of gross receipts on systems development and maintenance. At the same time, demand is increasing for experienced, competent people to do this work. James Martin, who has researched and written a great deal about information systems, estimates that the current unsatisfied demand for systems would keep existing development personnel busy for four years, and that this backlog has doubled in the last four years.

Finally, protection of the assets manipulated by EDP systems is largely dependent on the controls built into those systems. Thus, a generation of systems developers who are not attentive to loss control issues will create a generation of EDP systems in which loss control is not a primary objective. Indeed, this situation has already arisen and deserves urgent attention.

EDP Systems Development: Background

EDP systems development spans many activities performed by a variety of people. It usually starts with an operating manager or a process designer (a user) who has a problem—a process step that is too people-intensive, subject to error, boring to the point that worker turnover is high and product quality low, or simply impossible for an unaided human to perform reliably. The user often seeks a solution in an EDP system and calls in an EDP professional, a systems analyst. Together they define the user requirements in functional terms, stating *what* the system must do. The analyst then works with a system designer to prepare a design specification telling *how* the system will do it. A programmer translates the specification into a program, tests it, and then generally works with the systems analyst and the user to put it into operation in the business context.

For small systems requiring the investment of, say, fewer than six person-months, this is a relatively uncomplicated process. However, for more complex and broader systems needs, EDP technology offers more and more attractive opportunities and the process becomes vastly more involved. The accompanying tabulation presents the expanded number of stages in systems development projects. In this challenging environment, it is not uncommon in large companies to find systems development staffs of 300–400 professionals and single systems development projects involving fifty or one hundred person-years of effort.

Business systems development began as a process less than thirty years ago when General Electric acquired one of the first Univac I's for its small-appliance operation. Previously, what little computer work had been done was scientific or military in nature, and program specifications were purely mathematical. Attention was focused on writing programs and getting them to run reliably and correctly, and programming methods were primitive and error-prone. Not until the 1960s was systems development, as distinct from the programming process, recognized as a complex endeavor requiring a body of knowledge, methods, tools, and controls. Thus, systems developers and users today find themselves depending on a process only two decades old and one still widely considered to be more art than science. There are many excellent practitioners of the "art," but few have taken the view that it should be reduced to a science. On the other hand, many EDP professionals and business managers have come to support the view that business effectiveness demands that systems development be a science. One important advance in this direction has been the appearance of systems development methodologies.

Stages in Systems Development Projects

Stage	Function
Stage	*Function*
User requirements	Define need
System alternatives	Propose solutions
Feasibility study	Select optimum solution
Functional specification	Define system at "what" level
Design specification	Define system at "how" level
Programming	Prepare programs and conduct simple tests
System tests	Test programs against specification
Conversion/cutover	Prepare operating environment and install system
Acceptance	User "buys" system and initiates full operation
Post-implementation audit	Assess success of system

The Rise of Systems Development Methodologies

A systems development methodology is a body of procedures and supporting standards, formats, and processes designed to ensure a uniform, orderly, controlled approach to the entire life cycle of an EDP system. It is based on the division of that life cycle into stages, such as the one in the accompanying tabulation; often the stages are further subdivided. The methodology identifies these divisions of the life cycle with documentary and program products and describes the content and formats of the latter. Chief among these documents are feasibility studies, specifications, programs, and test plans. Progress from one stage to the next is generally contingent on formal reviews of the documents by EDP professionals, users, and audit staff. The purpose of this structure is to regularize the process, involve all appropriate people, and prevent oversights and omissions of vital steps.

Many systems development methodologies have been created and put into use by the larger or more advanced EDP organizations. Most of these have remained in-house methodologies. A few, however, are sold as commercial packages; Atlantic Software's SDM/70 is the most widely used. Many smaller companies have no formalized methodology for developing systems, and some companies do not carefully follow the ones they have.

Using a systems development methodology contributes to loss control in EDP systems. By imposing structure on the process, use of a methodology tends to improve its efficiency and effectiveness. This helps control the losses associated with ill-managed and poorly executed projects undertaken to develop new EDP systems. Some methodologies provide for some participation by internal auditors in the design process for two purposes: to help ensure that proper accounting controls are designed into the system, and to help ensure that cost-benefit considerations leading to the decision to create the system were properly studied and evaluated.

Finally, no systems development methodology that we know of deals directly with maintaining integrity of controls in existing systems undergoing maintenance or enhancement. Most companies, especially those not undergoing rapid change, spend more money on modifying existing systems than on building new ones. The modification of existing systems creates two possibilities, one a problem, the other an opportunity. The control structure of an existing system may be threatened by a change that is made in ignorance of its control objectives and logic. On the other hand, the upgrading of a system provides an occasion to consider improving its control integrity. This can be an expensive process, but in selected cases it deserves serious consideration.

In recent years many organizations have used an alternative in acquiring new systems capabilities—the selection and installation of software packages. Since the late 1960s, general-purpose software packages have become increasingly available for basic applications such as payroll, accounts receivable and payable, and general ledger. Although acquiring a package shortens the detail design and programming stages, much in-house work remains for the user and an EDP professional: they must still produce a functional specification and implement testing, conversion, and cutover. Thus, much of what is true for systems developed "from scratch" is also true when packages are involved. Packages, because they are intended for broad use and are generally thoroughly tested by many users, tend to have better internal controls than their unmarketed, privately developed counterparts. Nevertheless, determining control objectives, assessing control effectiveness, and ensuring control integrity remain the responsibility of the systems development team.

Loss Control and the Process of Systems Development

Loss control has a significant relationship to each of the three areas of systems development:

1. New systems
2. Existing systems
3. The systems development process

Although in all three areas the objective is to ensure that proper measures are taken to control losses, each presents different problems and involves different methods.

New systems: The inclusion of proper controls in a new system is best begun very early in its life cycle. The first step is to establish the system's control objectives. Almost as soon as the user and business systems analyst (see "What Is a Business Systems Analyst?") begin to establish the functional specifications of the system, they must also consider the questions of control. Typical questions include:

- What assets does the system manipulate?
- What threats are those assets subject to in the purview of this system's function?
- What are the likelihoods of those threats?
- What are the consequences if those threats eventuate?
- What level of protection is appropriate?

These are the fundamental questions of any risk analysis, and the answers define the system's control objectives.

Control objectives generally parallel the functional objectives. They should state in quantitative terms what guarantees of accuracy and completeness must be met about individual transactions and the totality of transactions in a processing run, and what safeguards should be installed against omitting or misperforming processing steps. Control objectives must consider both unintentional and intentional acts that threaten assets. ■ The following might be appropriate control objectives for a simple payroll system:

1. Additions, deletions, or other changes to employee pay records must be auditable and be authenticated by proper authority.
2. Employee pay records must be stored and maintained as confidential documents, with access restricted to a minimum number of people.
3. The probability of an undetected computational error must be exceedingly small.
4. Unusual values of pay or benefits or unusual activity patterns of individual employees or groups must be brought to management's attention.
5. The probability of an undetected failure to process an employee record must be exceedingly small.
6. The probability of an undetected loss or theft of checks or check stock must be exceedingly small.

As the functional design of a new system progresses, the user and the business systems analyst start to fulfill the control objectives by selecting and specifying various controls. For example, control objective 1 requires that additions, deletions, and other changes to the employee pay records be authorized and auditable. Assume that the system employs batch update of the records from information entered via data entry terminals in the payroll department. Then the user and the business systems analyst may decide upon the following as controls to meet the objective:

A. All changes must be recorded on a standard data entry form that carries an authorizing signature.

B. Prior to data entry, the forms must be reviewed for correctness by a personnel clerk who can verify the authenticity of the signature.

C. Data entry access must be controlled by locating the terminals in the payroll department, using passwords to control access by the data entry clerks, and using lockwords on the update and master files.

D. Employee pay records must contain at least one year's history of updates, including the serial number of the data entry sheet and the identity of the data entry operator.

This example deals with a very simple application operating in a simple environment. More realistically, an on-line order system, for example, will require careful consideration to prepare a suitable set of control objectives, and painstaking analysis to define the controls to carry out the objectives.

Dealing with each control objective in this way produces a structure of control for the entire proposed system. Like many other design endeavors, the process is iterative; meeting each objective generates new ideas for controls and suggests possible refinements of previous choices.

Three related questions also worth considering at a fairly early stage are:

- How can these controls be tested to ensure that they work when the system begins full-scale operation?
- How can these controls be verified to be working properly during the operational life of the system?
- How can an attempt at violation or a breakdown of the control be made known?

These are important considerations; a nonworking control is useless, an unverifiable control provides only uncertainty, and a control that does not announce its failure breeds a false sense of security. System testing must include explicit testing of all controls. This is a demanding requirement that is not often handled properly. All parties to the system development process need to put full attention into this effort.

It is also necessary to include mechanisms for control verification after cutover. These mechanisms generally take a form analogous to the "push-to-test" button on some electronic equipment. Some explicit test facility is provided, most often a preestablished set of input data with predictable results that can be run through the system, often in a somewhat unrealistic environment. Some of the input data are especially constructed to trigger operation of the controls; the remainder are designed to check basic operations of the system. ■ A worldwide manufacturer that both leases and sells its product tests its very complex accounts-receivable system with a collection of more than 30,000 dummy accounts embodying virtually all possible account conditions.

Existing systems: All existing systems enter the systems development process when they undergo change or enhancement. Modification may be as small as changing the value of a parameter (such as a change of the FICA deduction percentage in the payroll system) or as far-reaching as changing basic characteristics of the system (such as the introduction of some form of incentive pay into the payroll system). These modifications require some loss control steps analogous to those for new systems.

First, the functional character of the change must be evaluated in the light of the control objectives of the system. The system to be changed may have been developed under a methodology that did not provide for the explicit statement of control objectives. In this event, the user and the responsible business systems analyst should commit these objectives to writing in order to clarify their thinking about the change and its impact and to provide a resource for subsequent users and modifiers of the system. Any change that affects the control objectives must be examined. The proposed change must be rethought or objectives compromised. Failure to provide this kind of protection can reduce control integrity.

Next, features being added to the system must be analyzed in the same way that an entire new system is, and changes to existing features must be checked to ensure that controls associated with those features are not impaired. Detection of subtle forms of impairment may require substantial analysis by specialists. Sometimes a built-in control deficiency in the existing system becomes apparent during analysis of the proposed change. In general, retrofitting controls into existing systems is difficult and costly, but if it is really necessary, this may be the best time to do it. ■ One petroleum company has established a change control committee to pass on the control integrity of key application systems undergoing major change.

Finally, testing controls is as important for modified systems as for newly developed ones. The related requirement for control verification, which continues throughout the life of the system, may require enhanced provisions after the change.

The systems development process: Substantial amounts of money are spent to develop systems. As with any other business-related process, it is part of management's responsibility to ensure that assets are prudently expended. This means that EDP loss control must concern itself with the structure and conduct of the development process and the quality of its products.

Formalized systems development methodologies are important aids in achieving loss control goals. Most of these methodologies focus on the documentary products of the process, and on the reviews conducted to assess conformance of those documents to the standards established in the methodology. This arrangement provides an ideal vehicle for introducing the needs, techniques, and evaluations appropriate for effective loss control.

As the development project moves through its phases, the loss control team should address the following issues:

- Are the expected benefits commensurate with the expected cost?
- Does performance to date (in terms of schedule and budget conformance) indicate overall success?
- Do the results of conformance reviews of intermediate documentary products indicate adequate quality and control integrity in the final product?

If formalized systems development methodologies are not used, the questions remain the same but the answers are harder to obtain with any degree of certainty, and loss control in the systems development environment becomes more costly and less reliable. This reason alone should justify the acquisition and use of such methodologies in larger organizations, since those costs are relatively small compared to the overall development expenditures that are at risk. ■ An airline adopted a packaged systems development methodology in progressive fashion, applying it experimentally in one project and comparing results with a similar project conducted in the prevailing way. Results were encouraging and served to help build favorable staff opinion for full-scale cutover to the methodology.

The Roles of the Participants

Many interested parties are involved in systems development and each has something important to contribute, both in the basic design of the system and in supporting loss control objectives. The following discussion of the roles of these participants emphasizes the aspects of their roles that relate to EDP loss control. Table 4 summarizes these roles in conjunction with the stages of development.

The user: The user is the customer for the system under development and thus deserves to be listened to with attention and care, especially with regard to the issue of loss prevention. The user is usually the best available authority on the desired functional characteristics of the proposed system and on the

Table 4. *Roles of the participants in systems development*

Stages of development	Participants					
	User	*Business Systems Analyst*	*EDP Systems Designer*	*EDP Auditor*	*EDP Quality Assurer*	*Managers*
User requirements	Define loss control needs					Support, oversee, review
System alternatives		Propose controls				
Feasibility study		Assess control options		Advise on control options		
Functional specification	Define controls	Define controls		Review control structure		
Design specification			Implement controls →			
Programming						
Systems test						
Conversion/cutover	Verify controls	Verify controls		Review plan and controls	Consult on control implementation →	
Acceptance	Verify controls	Verify controls		Review plan and controls	Consult on control effectiveness →	
Post-implementation audit				Conduct		

What Is a Business Systems Analyst?

The business systems analyst is the bridge between the user and the EDP systems designer. Ideally, he or she knows the basic nature of the user's needs and business processes and is well versed in the array of capabilities available in the information systems function to deal with those needs and processes. The contribution of this person is truly multidisciplinary.

Only recently has this role been recognized as a necessary one. For many years, users dealt directly with EDP specialists. Often these specialists learned something about the user's problem and then went off and created a solution. More often than not, the solution solved a somewhat different problem from the one the user had articulated, and several iterations were required to come close to handling the actual business need. Today more and more organizations recognize the importance of the role of the business systems analyst in systems development and are benefiting from better systems, completed closer to schedule and budget.

---

assets being handled, the threats they are subject to, and the likelihoods that the threats will eventuate. Thus, the user should have a major hand in identifying and clarifying these issues both when the control objectives are set and when the control structure is in the initial stages of conception. The user can also offer advice as to the practicality of controls in the operating environment. This advice will help designers avoid formulating a control that is technically right but practically unfeasible. Finally, the user has a major role in planning and executing tests of the controls and in developing verification methods for them.

Many users, through pressures of their daily work, are reluctant to devote the time necessary to fulfill the role set forth. The other participants in system development must provide special encouragement for the user to adjust his or her priorities suitably.

The business systems analyst: Business systems analysts are members of a newly recognized profession, but their functions in controlling loss have been essential since the beginning of EDP systems development.

In loss control matters, the business systems analyst interacts with the user to clarify and make exhaustive the user's ideas about internal controls in the proposed system. ■ In the payroll example cited above, one control objective covered controlled access to the terminals used for data entry. In this case, the business systems analyst, working with the user, could be expected to define in substantial functional detail:

- How many terminals are needed
- What functions will be performed on the terminals that require controlled access
- Whether multiple levels of access control are required
- How passwords and lockwords will be employed to control access
- How issuance and change of passwords will be administered
- Whether encryption is appropriate
- How transaction authorization will take place

The business systems analyst uses knowledge of EDP capabilities to provide implementations for the requirements of loss control. Together the business systems analyst and the user produce a functional specification. This document tells *what* the new system is to do but not *how* it is to do it. The business systems analyst also takes the lead in defining the acceptance test that will be the final measure of whether the system works or not. In this test, verification of the presence and operability of internal controls is an important ingredient.

The EDP systems designer: The EDP systems designer applies expert knowledge of EDP systems technology to fulfill the requirements of the functional specification. Using this document as input, the designer creates an array of algorithms and data structures that models the requirements of the functional specification. These algorithms and data structures are described in a design specification, which tells how the procedural (computer, and sometimes person) level will carry out the requirements of the functional specification. This document in turn drives the programming and procedure-writing processes.

In addressing loss control, the EDP systems designer cooperates with the business systems analyst and, using control standards and guidelines, selects specific internal control algorithms—control totals, hash totals, encryption, and the like—for inclusion in the system. The designer also ensures that these internal controls will be "instrumented" in ways that will provide for simple and effective testing of their operability and integrity.

The EDP auditor: The EDP auditor plays an indirect role in creating the new system by reviewing the developing system and the project activities that create it.

In reviewing the developing system, the EDP auditor ensures that suitable controls are included in the system; reviews the testing, conversion, and acceptance processes; and ensures that the system is reviewed after implementation to lay the groundwork for constructive feedback of experience into controls selection. The EDP auditor interprets control standards for the user, business systems analyst, and EDP systems designer and offers advice on the general subject of controls selection. The EDP auditor also reviews the various products output from the systems development methodology, with special emphasis on the functional specification and the acceptance test procedures. As always, the EDP auditor must be careful to preserve the independence of the auditing function; she or he should avoid prescribing specific controls in the design and instead direct the developers' attention to requirements for control. As an aid to later auditing of the completed system when it reaches production status, the EDP auditor may request that certain features be included in the system design. To enhance audit independence, it is desirable to use different auditors to provide the design and post-implementation reviews.

The auditor contributes to the project activities of the development process itself by reviewing the project in terms of budget and schedule to make sure that the cost-benefit tradeoffs are in keeping with organization policy. In this role, the auditor fulfills for the development project the same role as for any other major project carried out by the organization, such as the construction of a building.

Others: Some EDP organizations have a quality assurance department which also plays a part in systems development. This department often serves an intermediary role between those of the EDP systems designer and the EDP auditor. When there is a suitable division of labor and responsibility between the EDP quality assurer and the EDP auditor, each can support the other and reinforce the integrity of controls in the developed systems product.

Managers in all of these areas must publicly endorse and visibly support the work of their subordinates in the systems development process.

CASE STUDY

Background

☐ A medium-sized supermarket chain, after many years of conservative management and slow growth, acquired a more aggressive and modern management team. Most departments, including EDP, had suffered from extremely tight budgets under the old management. Equipment and systems were antiquated, undocumented, and hopelessly patched.

As one part of a program of modernization, the new management resolved to increase the budget, management, technical skills, and consequently the performance level of the EDP department. It initiated a hiring program for both systems development and operations personnel, and top management mandated a program of modernization of all major systems.

Method

The new management retained a team of consultants to work with EDP in planning implementation of the mandate. The consultants reviewed the effectiveness of the major application systems and the degree of risk they posed to the company. They assigned priorities to the systems opportunities in light of the limited but growing resources of the EDP department and drew up a systems development plan for the next eighteen months.

The payroll system was the first one chosen for upgrading. The existing payroll system was a hand-me-down from the days of card-oriented systems and was full of special features to accommodate the wide variety of terms and conditions in the many different union contracts under which the clerks, butchers, truck drivers, and other hourly occupations worked. The system had no reliable documentation and could be operated by only two computer operators (both unionized employees) who had learned it "by heart." For these reasons, all relating more to risk than to effectiveness, payroll became the leading edge of the modernization effort.

Because of the basic character of the payroll application, and because the need for improvement was urgent, the consultants recommended the purchase of a software package from a nationally known vendor. Implementation of the package was turned over to the EDP department, working with the vendor's field staff. The EDP department had never installed a package before and because of rapid growth had many new members who were unsure of the company's methods and needs. The payroll department was not skilled in EDP techniques, and there was nobody who could serve as business systems analyst, with the possible exception of one senior member of the vendor's staff. That person had little time to spend with the user and was more anxious to "sell" the package than to solve all of the payroll department's problems.

The undermanned and overworked internal audit department had no capability to audit either EDP operations or development. Due to lack of resources it declined to review the internal controls in the recommended package. No corresponding offer was made to the department concerning the development/installation process.

The consultants had left a detailed plan for implementation of the payroll package. This plan included consultation with the user and formulation of a functional specification for the parts of the package that had to be customized to the needs of the company. These were mostly front-end features, such as time-card formats and procedures, special terms of certain union contracts, and all of the procedures for converting from the existing system to the new system. Although the EDP department had no standard systems development methodology to guide it through the process, the plan had the potential to serve as a methodology for the project.

Results

Inevitably problems delayed the completion of intermediate products, but management refused to delay introduction of the new system. Over time the schedule and the project managers became less and less realistic and drastically reduced the time allowed for testing and for training of payroll personnel in order to hold to the implementation date.

One prerequisite for use of the new system was the conversion of the payroll master file into the format of the new system. At this stage the payroll package software proved the value of some of its controls. The conversion program made several consistency and redundancy checks on the employee files it processed. The conversion program found that more than 3 percent of the employee records were erroneous or incomplete and that another 1 percent were downright suspicious. In this category were multiple records under the same name but with different social security numbers. This turned out to be a device (set up with connivance of a payroll clerk) for older part-time employees receiving social security benefits to avoid the reduction in benefits resulting from excess earnings. There were also several records for employees who had been discharged as much as two years before, and one record for an unknown "employee" in a fictitious department. Some of the latter records were the result of human error, but in a few cases, investigation disclosed that time cards had been turned in and checks issued and cashed.

The conversion process itself went raggedly. Controls on the data input from time cards were poorly enforced because the payroll clerks had not been adequately trained. As a result, some erroneous checks were issued, and the payroll department heard only about the checks that were too small. Controls on output suffered from the same kind of difficulties. In general, however, the high level of internal controls built into the package by the professional designers paid dividends in improved integrity and reliability and in confidence in the system. Most of the difficulties came from the portions of the package and procedures that were customized by the EDP department to fit the needs of the company.

Conclusions

The EDP department reviewed the process after the majority of problems in the implementation had been worked out. They highlighted the following as mistakes to be avoided in the subsequent stages of their eighteen-month plan:

- They had not allowed enough time to define thoroughly the special needs of the payroll department. They resolved to pay the package vendor for additional services to ensure that all the user's needs were identified and satisfactorily dealt with in the customizing process next time.

- They had not had enough input from auditors on the matter of internal controls in the parts of the system that they had developed themselves. If the internal audit department could not help them, they decided to hire outside consultants for help.
- They had not had enough objective appraisal of the development process to ensure that the project proceeded with sufficient care and low risk. Subsequent projects would be reviewed by a management oversight committee including representation from the user, the internal audit department, and from a yet-to-be formed EDP quality assurance department.

On the other hand, the EDP department recognized the value of the risk analysis process that had targeted the payroll system as the first candidate for upgrading. It planned to use the same approach in evaluating future systems opportunities and in periodically reevaluating the priorities already set. The department came to appreciate the value of a standard systems development methodology and began an effort to select one of the packaged methodologies on the market. □

Evaluate the Scope of Participation
in Systems Development in Your Organization

1. Select two or three representative projects from recent systems development projects in your organization. If possible, choose a fairly large one, involving a minimum of two or three person-years; another addressed to the enhancement of an existing system; and, if possible, one involving the acquisition of packaged software.
2. Obtain documentation on the projects, including both documentary products (such as specifications and test plans), and project documents (such as budgets and progress reports).
3. From the documentation, reconstruct the history of the projects, correlating the documents with the systems development project stages listed above.
4. Determine the extent to which participants fulfilled the roles recommended in table 4.
5. Obtain from users, from records of changes made to the systems after installation, and from loss reports any data or opinions about the demonstrated control integrity of the developed systems.
6. Obtain from project participants and from project records any data and opinions about the budget and schedule conformance of the development projects.
7. From the information gathered in steps 4, 5, and 6 formulate tentative conclusions regarding control of losses in systems development and in the developed systems.

A Perspective on Chapter 9

Smith has reviewed the performance of his organization and used the results to guide his future actions. (From "The Wizard of ID," by Brant Parker and Johnny Hart. By permission of Johnny Hart and Field Enterprises, Inc.)

9

Conduct Comprehensive Periodic Program Reviews

This chapter describes the final step in effective EDP loss control—looking at what has been done and acting upon the results of that review. Here we examine the planning and objective setting for such reviews, discuss the key attributes of successful reviews, and present the steps involved in a typical review.

In setting the organizational context for EDP loss control, we presented a mnemonic (GOSPEL) in chapter 1 to represent the six steps in the strategic business process. The last two letters stand for Evaluation and Looping—that is, measuring results and feeding back the measurements in the form of corrections to the upstream portions of the process. The same activities are called for in reviewing programs, and the same type of benefits accrue. The chief benefit is that the EDP loss control program becomes more effective, in the sense that it is directed toward doing the *right* tasks. The review process identifies particularly productive and unproductive activities and diagnoses the reasons for their characteristic performance. The result is to accentuate the positive, eliminate the negative. ■ During a review of its loss control program, a major West Coast bank detected significant improvements in the number of systems development projects being completed on time and on budget. The review team found evidence of a connection between these results and the use of a formal systems development methodology that had hitherto been in only limited use. The team recommended, and management mandated, wider use of the methodology.

The EDP loss control program also becomes more efficient: results are achieved with less effort because inefficient methods are identified and can be improved. Finally, review increases awareness of the need for EDP loss control and the disciplines it entails, with attendant benefits through prevention and deterrence of acts that may produce losses. ■ The second periodic review of the loss control program at a large oil company showed improvement in password discipline among the several hundred time-sharing users in the company. Part of this improvement was attributed to education and enforcement processes, part to increased awareness resulting from the reviews themselves.

This chapter emphasizes the comprehensive and periodic nature of loss control program reviews. No important aspect of the program should go unevaluated. Periodic reviews ensure that problems do not become too large before detection. Satisfying these requirements demands a significant allocation of program resources to this function—probably 5 or 10 percent of overall resources—but this is money well spent in the cause of future improvement in performance and avoidance of future costs.

Planning the EDP Loss Control Program Review

To yield the highest benefits, a carefully reasoned review plan is essential. The loss control program review is a typical example of a "study"—an endeavor to obtain useful answers to a problem or set of problems. As such, those planning the review can benefit from the basic study-planning approach developed in the scientific and business worlds, described opposite.

The first step, defining the issues, is critical to the success of the review process. Study staff must ask themselves two searching questions and seek their answers:

A. What are management's prime concerns about EDP-related losses?

B. What are management's prime expectations for the program?

■ The management of an airline commissioned a review of its data processing function and directed that the study examine closely the vulnerability of its computer facility. Since the survival of the airline depended entirely on its ability to sell seats through its computerized reservation system, this strong focus on one aspect of EDP loss control was entirely appropriate. The issue was straightforward: Was the company accepting an improper amount of risk, and what were the alternatives?

■ In a bank undertaking a program review, the review team addressed the first question by giving management a list of possible concerns and then asking: "If you lost 100 minutes of sleep over EDP loss control, how many minutes would be lost for each of the concerns on the list (or ones you might add)?"

Determining the answers to the two questions above is tantamount to understanding what issues drive the review process. If the review does not deal directly with the issues, its results and recommendations are not very likely to be accepted by management and implemented.

The Purpose of the Review Process

Common sense dictates that any really productive review process have three related generic objectives:

1. Ascertain current status: What are we doing?
2. Measure effectiveness: How are we doing?
3. Provide feedback: How can we do better in the future?

Experience with EDP loss control programs and with other programs intended to have an impact on behavior indicates that well-conducted pro-

---

Issues and Answers

A political-interview TV show uses the title, "Issues and Answers" presumably to emphasize the public's desire to get answers to political questions of major scope. However, issues and answers also have broader applicability. Any study such as an EDP loss control program review benefits from careful planning to ensure that the right questions are asked, the right sources of information chosen, the right analytical methods used, and the right conclusions drawn. Many consultants and professional problem solvers use the following model:

1. Identify the issues—the fundamental questions and concerns that are being asked by the commissioners and beneficiaries of the study.
2. Analyze the issues to derive a small number of concrete objectives for the study.
3. Define a set of deliverables—the "hard" products that will contain the answers sought.
4. Identify the data sources necessary to feed into the deliverables.
5. Identify the analysis methods necessary to process the data in order to produce the deliverables.
6. Organize the activities necessary to create the deliverables. The activities should form a series of logically interconnected tasks.
7. Determine the amount of resources and time needed to perform the tasks and prepare the deliverables.

If the pattern shown above is followed carefully, your organization should be able to follow through each of the steps, picking out for each of the issues the objectives, deliverables, data, analysis methods, tasks, costs, and time needed to obtain the answers to each issue. The ability to thread one's way consistently and logically from issues to answers is the criterion of a good study plan.

---

gram reviews have a bonus value: they heighten awareness of the program and its purposes, methods, and results. Because of this bonus value, an additional program review objective should be:

4. Increase awareness: How can we involve the broadest group of people?

These four generic objectives must be interpreted in the light of the issues determined in the first step of the review planning process. Emphasize program activities that rank highest in management's concern, not just because management is the boss but because it is charged with interpreting and carrying out corporate objectives and programs and therefore is responsible for directing resource allocation throughout the organization.

Ascertain current status: Determining current status is a fairly straightforward investigative and reportorial task, and familiar methods apply and are effective. The crucial decision here relates to scope. Especially if the EDP loss control program is a broad one, the objective should be interpreted in relation to the individual elements of the program and to the investment, importance, and expected payoffs of those elements. ■ A large computer manufacturer concentrates a significant part of its EDP loss control expenditures on control of configuration changes in critical application software and a proportionate amount on program review of these efforts.

Measure effectiveness: Setting detailed objectives for measuring effectiveness is logically coupled to the assessment of current status. These objectives must also specify the degree of accuracy, timeliness, and quantitativeness of measures. ■ In reviewing the loss reporting aspects of the program in a large financial services company, the review planner set objectives for measuring the correctness of information in the loss reports, the completeness of the reports, the timeliness of data and of delivery, and the size of the sample of reports reviewed.

Provide feedback: Detailed objectives for providing feedback should concern themselves with sharpening the focus and direction of the ongoing elements of the program. It may be necessary to assess what information a particular program element lacks for effective direction and to direct the review process toward acquiring the necessary data. ■ In the loss reporting example above, two objectives of the review were to verify the utility of the data items included in the loss report and to investigate the desirability of adding other data items.

Increase awareness: The planner of the EDP loss control program review should set detailed objectives to involve the broadest spectrum of organization groups practicable. He or she should aim for breadth of participation in review tasks and specify the widest possible dissemination of results. ■ In reviewing the program element relating to loss reporting, the planner at the large financial services company listed both the reporting agencies to be interviewed and the recipients of the evaluation segment dealing with loss reporting.

Key Attributes of an EDP Loss Control Program Review

Common sense, experience, and good management practice suggest that to ensure the validity and acceptance of results and to provide a smooth and efficient review, the review process must have four attributes:

1. Appropriate participants
2. Appropriate timing
3. Appropriate charter, responsibility, and authority
4. Appropriate dissemination of results

Participants: To be an appropriate participant in the EDP loss control program review, a candidate must be able to contribute information, objectivity, understanding, and credibility. Possible candidates include:

- EDP loss control program representative
- EDP operations representative
- EDP systems development representative
- EDP quality assurance representative
- EDP user representatives
- Internal audit representative
- External auditor
- Loss control consultant
- General management representatives, chosen from:
    Security
    Insurance administration
    Controller
    Treasurer
    Operating managers

These participants are not all expected to be full-time reviewers. They should devote only as much time as they can while still performing their regular duties. The review leader should carefully plan these review activities and see that they are carried out. All participants should have a clearly defined responsibility, a schedule for fulfilling it, and a meaningful role in producing the final review report. Their help must be sought, their opinions listened to, their contributions included in the result, and their approval of the final product secured. ■ A medium-sized midwestern utility formed a team to review its loss control program. The team was led by the EDP operations manager and included the manager of systems development, a technically oriented analyst, an EDP auditor, and the corporate manager of security and safety. Later a loss control consultant reviewed the team report and generally approved the conclusions but pointed out the absence of any user representatives on the team.

Timing: For the timing of reviews, two approaches are in use. The simpler but sometimes more demanding one is a simultaneous review of all aspects of the EDP loss control program. In a small organization this is fairly easy to do without disruption of other activities, because the review does not require much time from the participating agencies. An annual review in the second fiscal quarter usually works out well, because year-end closing is complete, annual data are available, and participants are likely to have more time available.

The alternative is to review elements of the program one at a time throughout the year. This approach requires more administration but offers more flexibility. It also offers the opportunity to review elements on various frequencies—critical elements can be reviewed every six months, normal elements every year, and noncritical elements every eighteen months to two years. ■ One multinational manufacturer uses an innovative modification of this approach, dividing the review task between company staff and the external auditor. Each takes half of the program each review period and exchanges halves for the next periodic review.

Charter, responsibility, and authority: The EDP loss control program review has many of the characteristics of an audit: the review team must have unrestricted access to information, sufficient resources to do its job, and a clear channel to top management. The best way of ensuring these is to provide the review team with a written charter, an explanation of the responsibility and authority of the team, and an endorsement of the activity by top management. ■ One organization with a particularly strong internal audit department couples the loss control program review with the regular internal audit program of the company. Internal audit leads reviews and enlists substantial assistance from the EDP group's specialists for the duration of the review.

The review team should have an organizational structure of its own, with a team leader chosen and properly supported by management. Choosing the leader from outside the loss control program staff often works well, especially if an enthusiastic user or financial staff member can be found. Rotating leadership on successive reviews is desirable. Appointment of task leaders to deal with portions of the review is also effective, especially if the review is an extensive one.

Dissemination of results: The dissemination of the results of an EDP loss control review operates under two conflicting pressures. The foremost consideration is the potential sensitivity of the results. If the review identifies a vulnerability of significant proportions, it clearly is not appropriate to disseminate such information widely, lest someone take advantage of the vulnerability before it can be corrected. The review may identify substandard performance in certain program elements. The normal approaches used in reporting and correcting deficiencies found in financial audits work well in this case.

   On the other hand, broad dissemination of results increases the organization's awareness of the importance of EDP loss control. At the minimum, successes identified by the review should receive wide publicity and praise. Highly rated individuals, groups, and departments deserve recognition, which will inspire effort by others. ■ Several companies use their company newsletter for this purpose; one company uses its loss control periodical to publish summarized review results. Chapter 6 discusses additional approaches.

How to Conduct the Review

The review itself consists of seven steps, which for the most part are accomplished serially:

1. Agree on purpose and scope.
2. Select documents and activities to be reviewed.
3. Gather data.
4. Analyze data.
5. Formulate conclusions.
6. Develop recommendations and an action plan
7. Prepare the final report.

   Each step is a vital part of a successful review and deserves careful attention.

Agree on purpose and scope: First analyze the issues and set the objectives of the review. Communicate these objectives to the review team and secure their inputs and agreement on the purposes of the review and the scope of activities. This process requires constructive interaction. The leader must meet with the team, establish a constructive atmosphere, offer the initial plan, and solicit ideas. At this stage it is important to listen carefully and sympathetically, analyze collectively with the other members, and write down and circulate the agreements that result. If events during the review create pressures to deviate from the agreement, these pressures should be dealt with openly and jointly, but with the team leader assuming leadership responsibility.

Select documents and activities to be reviewed: If the objectives and scope of the review have been well defined, the selection of documents and activities almost executes itself. Identify the documents input to and output from the program elements and examine them for applicability. The natural candidates for review of operations are the functional activities that produce, alter, maintain, read, analyze, and otherwise use the selected documents. Then select key individuals to interview and key operational elements to audit.

Gather data: Once the target documents, individuals, and operations are identified, gather the necessary data. Take careful notes during interviews and transcribe the notes into final form as soon thereafter as possible. Identify document sources, copy the documents for inclusion in working papers, and return the originals. If a large number of documents is to be collected, consider forming a central library for reference purposes. When you observe operations, take notes, collect sample documents, and verify use of policies, guidelines, and the like. Emphasize maintaining an audit trail that will allow the source and content of any fact to be verified.

Analyze data: Assemble and collate the data in some suitable, natural order, such as by department, application system, or type of control involved. Some analysis of raw data may be necessary to measure performance and trends. Preserve all raw data and any resulting computation sheets. Keep notes on the rationale for the selection of analytical methods.

Formulate conclusions: Keep conclusions distinct from the data and analyses that led up to them and from any recommendations that may result. Develop conclusions about each program element separately, then examine them as a whole. New insights often result from the apparent similarities or differences. Examine the conclusions in team meetings; make the proposer of the conclusion defend his position by offering evidence: keep asking "So what?" until you receive a solid answer. Management is likely to remain skeptical about some of the conclusions unless you are prepared to defend their accuracy. Seven elements are helpful in strengthening and illuminating conclusions:

- Results of previous reviews
- Research findings from the literature
- Industry checklists

- Scenarios of potential threats
- Tests of control procedures
- Threat analyses
- Experts to analyze special problems

Finally, develop some structure for the conclusions. Look for unifying ideas, common problems, and common successes.

Develop recommendations and an action plan: Once the conclusions are complete and buttressed with facts, recommendations will often flow almost automatically. Organize the recommendations by affected area so that it is clear who has the responsibility for implementation, then assign implementation priorities to each recommendation. A rough high/medium/low measure may be sufficient at first. Make rough estimates of the resources necessary to implement the recommendations, and develop a tentative schedule for implementation. List the benefits versus time, and list the risks that will result if the recommendations are not implemented. ■ A midwestern bank used the rough measures "high," "medium," and "low" for estimating resources required to effect the recommendations. The choice was based on the level of staff required *or* the approximate dollar cost for capital expenditures and staff time but not computer time. The specific relationship used was: low—less than three staff months or less than $12,000; medium—three to twelve staff months or $12,000–$50,000; high—more than twelve staff months or over $50,000.

Prepare the final report: Capsulize the purpose and scope of the review, the conclusions, recommendations, any minority report, and action plan and its supporting considerations in a formal executive summary report. Include in appendixes lists of documents, individuals, activities reviewed, and a breakdown of the team composition and responsibilities. Distribute the final report as widely as is consonant with sensitivity considerations.

The final report also serves an interesting secondary purpose: it is the basic vehicle by which the review process itself may be reviewed, by external and internal audit, management, and other interested parties.

CASE STUDY

Background

☐ Over a three-year period a large, multiplant manufacturer of replacement auto parts had instituted several elements of an EDP loss control program. Until recently all data processing had been centralized, with only shop floor data collection systems, limited data entry, and remote printing facilities at outlying plants. A loss reporting system was in operation, as was an access control system for the central computer facility and for the remote job entry facilities at the plants. Control standards had recently been developed and were being tested by the systems development group attached to the finance department. Risk analysis had been discussed but nothing significant done. There was no full-time head of the EDP loss control program; the director of computer operations filled the job as an additional duty. The ongoing loss control activities had never been independently evaluated. When the company decided to install some distributed data processing capability, the corporate officer to whom EDP reported suggested an EDP loss control program review.

Method

The corporate officer to whom EDP reported assigned a plant controller as the leader of the review team and gave him authority to deal with the EDP group and the various users on loss control matters. A general memorandum announced the appointment and described the purpose of the review, emphasizing its constructive nature.

The review team leader spent about a month educating himself on the general subject of EDP loss control, familiarizing himself with the general outlines of the loss control program, developing a plan with the aid of an informal advisory group, and securing his superior's approval. He made informal contacts with people he considered good candidates for the review team, and he identified a loss control consultant to function as his adviser. After securing approval of his candidates, the team leader conducted a series of planning meetings with the whole group. The team defined separate task groups to deal with:

1. Access controls at the central facility
2. Systems development controls
3. Internal controls in computer operations
4. Loss reporting systems at the central facility
5. Activities at the remote sites.

Working from outlines prepared in committee, each task group began its work. The group assigned to review the remote sites chose four major plants and visited each for three or four days. The other task groups scheduled their activities over a period of about one month.

After gathering the data, each task group formulated tentative conclusions and circulated them to the other members of the team. The team met to discuss and polish its conclusions and then solicited comments from the organizations under review on the correctness of the data and the conclusions drawn. Once the conclusions were confirmed, the recommendations and action plan were developed in joint meetings. The team leader prepared a draft of the final report, secured recommendations from the team members, and published the report.

Results

In general the review found the loss control program to be effective. The physical access controls on the central computer facility were rated highly, and physical access controls in the remote sites were rated fair to excellent. Logical access controls such as passwords, lockwords, and account identifiers were in daily use and were effectively administered, enforced, and protected. The computer center was following prescribed procedures for creating and maintaining on-site and off-site backup files. However, although the review generally approved the disaster plan, investigation revealed that the plan had not been tested since its preparation more than two years before.

The review team also examined two large and critical systems development projects currently under way. In each project existing standards for the inclusion of internal controls had been shortcut, with limited time and funds given as the reason. Both projects were behind schedule and were likely to overrun their budgets. The review concluded that there seemed to be insufficient attention to the practices of project management, especially in the close monitoring of progress versus expenditure.

The loss reporting system seemed to be working well. Managers reported that the very existence of the system had increased personnel's awareness of management's concern. The review team concluded that all associated with the system were using it conscientiously and that its data had provided some useful insights. In particular, analysis of reports of adjustments input to the computer-based product inventory system led to the elimination of certain careless product accounting practices in the warehouses of two plants. Similarly, analysis of reports of nonroutine shipping costs (categorized as EDP-related losses because the shipments were scheduled by manually overriding computer-produced plans) pinpointed certain lax practices in an outlying distribution point.

The review criticized the lack of an organized risk management process. Limited time and resources, however, prevented the team from specifying any unreasonable risks currently being borne by the company. The team recommended another review in one year, when "smart" terminals and other distributed processing capabilities would be in place in all plants to ensure that the loss control program would keep pace with technological changes. Because the loss control program was growing and would soon require full-time attention from a program director, the review also recommended that responsibility for loss control be transferred from the director of computer operations to someone else.

Conclusions

The corporate officer who had commissioned the review was generally satisfied with both the process and the result. He learned that EDP-related risks in several major areas were under control. The vital records of the company in the custody of the EDP department were well protected, both from deliberate or unintentional damage and from loss through disaster. The EDP loss reporting system was achieving some of its potential for improving operations and avoiding future losses. The problems identified in systems development served as a justification for allocating more management attention and resources to that area. Finally, the officer recognized the value of reviews and resolved to schedule one annually thereafter. □

A Look at Issues

Seeing other people's viewpoints is one of the hardest things to do and requires a lot of practice. Try the following:

1. Imagine that you are a member of the audit committee of the board of directors of your company. Write down what you think should be your responsibilities in that position. How do these responsibilities relate to EDP loss control? What would you like to know about EDP loss control activities in your company? Recall your obligations under the Foreign Corrupt Practices Act.
2. Imagine that you are the senior vice-president of finance. How are your responsibilities related to EDP loss control? What would you like to know about EDP loss control activities?
3. Repeat step 2 for the director of internal audit.
4. Repeat step 2 for the director of EDP.
5. Repeat step 2 for the external auditor.
6. Use the results of steps 1 through 5 to prepare a concise list of issues for an EDP loss control program review.
7. Use the list of issues to build a set of objectives for the review.
8. Carry on the review planning as far as you can.

A Perspective on Chapter 10

There are no "preservatives" that will keep vulnerable EDP assets protected while you make up your mind whether to start improving control over EDP-related losses in your organization. (From "Frank and Ernest," by Bob Thaves. Reprinted by permission. Copyright © 1981 NEA, Inc.)

10

Some Closing Words

Starting is something like going on a diet: there is no question but that it is good for you, yet somehow it seems that it is better to start next Monday, or the first of next month. In the meantime, the likelihood of serious consequences is probably very small. All of us know the fallacies of this argument, but many of us fall prey to them just the same. To get over this hump, review the steps laid out in the preceding nine chapters, assess the general level of control and vulnerabilities in your organization, and then get down to improving the control over EDP-related losses in your organization without delay.

A few down-to-earth principles will help. First, there is no magic involved, just hard work by managers and staff. Second, keep loss control in the proper perspective; it is an important part of the business, but it should not override other important considerations. Third, do not overreact to stories in the media; they may very well be inaccurate and sensationalized, and in any case they deal with an environment different from yours. Publicized EDP loss events can be useful spurs to self-examination, but they are poor foundations on which to base immediate action. Fourth, develop a plan and stick to it. Finally, think about loss control in a positive sense, as an important part of the stewardship of organization assets that is the responsibility of every manager; it is not "cops and robbers."

Putting These Ideas to Work in Your Organization

Foundations: Chapter 1 identified the first step in EDP loss control as establishing the proper corporate attitude. Without this, the loss control pro-

---

Remember

1. Hard work is required—there is no magic involved.
2. Keep a business perspective.
3. Do not overreact.
4. Develop and stick to a plan.
5. Think positively about loss control.

---

gram will make little progress. Also essential is the proper attitude in the person who leads the effort. In our experience, that person will be most successful if he or she understands and believes in the following principles:

- A constructive rather than authoritarian or punitive approach to dealing with people, organizations, and organizational problems and opportunities
- The ability of people, given proper incentives, to accomplish substantial personal and organizational change
- The applicability and effectiveness of good general management principles and practices to a variety of new situations, including EDP loss control
- The long-term worth of EDP loss control.

We have discussed concepts like these more than once before in this book. Cynics labeling them as "motherhood and apple-pie" may diminish their impact on managers who are concerned with loss control. That tendency is regrettable and must be resisted. The fact is that EDP loss control is a people problem and thus presents managers with a people opportunity. No wonder, then, that loss control problems respond best to people-oriented solutions. EDP frauds and defalcations are rarely committed by hardened criminals; more often they are perpetrated by ordinary people who see the criminal act as the only feasible solution to some major problem in their life, usually a problem that they feel unable to share with someone else. Penalties do not seem to loom large in their minds: they expect to commit the illegal act only once and get away with it. Solutions must therefore address the attitudes and actions of the potential perpetrator first, and build defenses around assets second. Errors and omissions that cause EDP-related losses are also people-dependent. An error of a computer operator or of a computer programmer that triggers a loss stems from personal attitude, motivation, education, training, loyalty, or relationship to supervisor or subordinate. Even losses due to natural causes have a human element. Although the loss control program cannot predict and forestall a flood, fire, or earthquake, that program can build attitudes and organize planned responses among personnel that will ameliorate the harmful consequences.

Priorities: The nine steps outlined in this book provide a good general framework, but every organization must decide which organizational function and element deserves priority of attention and resources. Generally there is much more to be done than there are resources immediately available. Some basic factors, however, can guide resource allocation decisions in your organization.

The two prerequisites are establishing the right corporate attitude toward EDP loss control and involving an auditing function (internal or external). With these as a foundation, the organization can prepare a loss control program, taking into consideration the following observations in setting priorities for program actions.

Almost without exception, ensuring continuity of the data processing activity is of first importance. Unless it is clear that necessary and sufficient measures have already been taken for physical and data security, these areas should be allocated enough resources to bring them up to a demonstrably suitable level. Security considerations should include attention to basic data control in computer operations, and logical access control by means of passwords and other access control techniques. Disaster recovery is a complex and demanding area that should be postponed until competence and confidence are firmly established.

Once all appropriate measures have been taken to provide adequate physical and data security, attention should turn to activities associated with development of new application systems and with maintenance of existing systems. This can begin at a fairly low level, but some continuing commitment should be made as early as possible. Much of the loss control effort directed to existing systems is required because those systems were developed without appropriate consideration of loss control issues. The commitment of resources to systems under development and modification minimizes the need for later attention by operating in a preventive rather than corrective mode.

In parallel with this activity, and also at a fairly low level to begin with, it is prudent to begin work in loss reporting and in asset and threat identification. These activities build the data base necessary to direct resources more effectively to future EDP loss control. These activities have a delayed payoff: it takes months and sometimes years to cover enough of the organization to realize the potential value of the effort. But if they are not started, they will never fulfill that potential.

Next, it is important to address the adequacy of controls in critical application systems. If suitable control standards exist, they can form the jumping-off point for review of application systems that handle the major assets of the organization. If not, resources must be allocated to the development of standards, but some review of the key applications should proceed on the basis of generally accepted control standards.

Training and professional development are a continuing priority. As mentioned earlier, 5 to 7 percent of the audit budget should be allocated for

EDP auditor training, with a somewhat smaller allocation to loss control training of data processors and managers. The level of knowledge and awareness in the organization will determine the specific priority.

Finally, set aside a small amount of time and resources, almost from the beginning, to review the progress of the other activities. Chapter 9 suggests approaches.

The size of the organization: EDP loss control is not just for the large organization with a big investment in EDP and many application systems handling major assets. Risks in middle-sized or small companies are indeed smaller in scale, but they should not be measured in absolute dollars. Rather, risks should be evaluated in terms of absolute dollars divided by the assets or sales of the company and in terms of the importance of the EDP resource to the continued existence of the company. If loss of the EDP resource for a short period can put a company out of business permanently, the organization must deal with that threat as a priority. Also, if a loss occurs, its impact is more likely to be felt in proportion to the reduction in earnings per share than in simple dollars.

On the other hand, it may be more difficult to get a commitment of resources to EDP loss control in a small company than in a large one, for a variety of reasons. In that case the manager concerned with loss control must simply treat the situation as an added problem, not as an excuse for abandoning efforts. That manager may have to make some compromises and to sharpen some priorities at the expense of others, but the stakes are proportionately just as high as if he were in the Fortune 500.

Loss Control Costs versus Benefits

Following the recommendations of this book will certainly mean that most organizations will spend more money on activities related to loss control. These costs will be clearly identifiable in the form of hours of staff time diverted from other, more routine activities. In some instances additional staff will be required to carry out these duties, and direct expenses (computer time, training courses, and the like) will be incurred for specific loss control activities.

The benefits resulting from these costs are not easy to list on a balance sheet, put in your pocket, or spend in the marketplace. Most are measurable in a negative way—generally by the absence or reduced frequency of occurrence of a harmful event. Because such events occur irregularly and infrequently, it is difficult to be sure that loss control activities are effective unless they are measured over a long time or are compared with many other similar situations.

Some measurable positive changes do result from a program of loss control, however, and they correlate well with the expectation of benefits. The success of activities directed to improving security awareness and loss control practices among staff can be measured by questionnaires, interviews, and observation. Loss reporting systems, once established, build a history that can be analyzed with growing confidence over time. Subjective estimates of the level of internal control integrity in application systems can be made, and a substantial degree of confidence attained that those estimates will correlate well with lowered susceptibility to loss.

Costs and benefits in EDP loss control have to be treated probabilistically, in much the same way that decisions are made regarding insurance. Costs associated with loss control are, in effect, insurance premiums; benefits are delivered in the form of reduced vulnerability to events that are beyond direct control. The cost-benefit equation makes good business sense only if the managers charged with the protection of the stakeholders' interests can justify the expenditure of the premiums in the light of the possible losses resulting from the otherwise unreduced vulnerabilities.

Thus, an organization undertaking a program of EDP loss control can expect to spend additional money to implement that program and in the short term will probably not be able to show any compensating gains from the expense. In the longer term, however, the program will affect the attitudes and behavior of staff, the general quality and control integrity of application systems, and the efficiency and quality of the application systems development process. These effects will all be positive, in the sense that the cost of doing business in the EDP area will be reduced and the quality of products and services improved. These long-term effects may offset the costs of the program, leaving a net benefit in the form of reduced risk of loss from intentional and unintentional acts. Thus it is most cost effective to start on this course of action as soon as possible. In the words of the cartoon, "Don't dawdle!"

As managers dedicated to the use of quantitative methods, we would like to be able to test thoroughly the accuracy of our claims in the preceding paragraph. The expense, uncertainty, and potentially disastrous results of a controlled comparison of two organizations, one with and one without an EDP loss control program, make this idealized type of test impractical. However, our experience and that of other practitioners in the field clearly indicate that the kind of loss control program we have described in this book is a good investment for any organization dependent on EDP systems and technology.

Bibliography

Sources include listings from "Computer Security Publications," National Bureau of Standards List No. 91, revised December, 1979; Peter Browne, "Computer Security—A Survey," Proceedings of the National Computer Conference, 1976; *SHARE—Security Blanket*; Computer Security Institute newsletter. Price and address information are based on mid-1982 data.

Periodicals

Assets Protection Journal is published every other month and covers criminalistics, legal issues, terrorism, computer security, training and new products. Annual subscriptions: $24. Available from Assets Protection, Suite 503, 500 Sutter Street, San Francisco, CA 94102.

Computer Fraud and Security Bulletin is a monthly newsletter published in England for computer security administrators. It identifies many computer crimes. Annual subscription: $55. Available from Elsevier International Bulletins, Mayfield House, 256 Banbury Road, Oxford OX2 7DH, England.

Computer Law and Tax Report, a monthly report by Robert P. Bigelow, concentrates on the legal implications of computer use with emphasis on privacy and security. Annual subscription: $58; 8 pages. Available from Warren Gorham and Lamont, 210 South Street, Boston, MA 02111.

Computer/Law Journal is a quarterly law journal devoted to computer technology law. Annual subscription: $60. Available from Center for Computer/Law, P.O. Box 54308 T.A., Los Angeles, CA 90054.

Computer Security is a bimonthly publication available with membership in the Computer Security Institute, Five Kane Industrial Drive, Hudson, MA 01749.

Computer Security Journal is published twice a year by the Computer Security Institute. Each issue contains over 100 pages of in-depth, state-of-the-art papers emphasizing practical application of topics from all areas of computer security. Annual subscription: $35, with discounts for CSI members.

The EDP Auditor is a quarterly magazine published by the EDP Auditors Association. Written for the EDP auditor, it concentrates on education and research. Annual subscription: $20, or as part of an annual membership in the EDP Auditors Association; membership dues vary depending on the local chapter. Also included in the membership is a quarterly "house organ" newsletter, *EDP Auditor Update*. Available from Administrative Office, EDP Auditors Association/Foundation, 373 S. Schmale Road, Carol Stream, IL 60187.

EDPACS (EDP, Audit, Control, and Security) is a monthly publication written with the auditor in mind but offers a great deal of useful information for anyone with computer security responsibility. Annual Subscription: $48; 20 pages. Available from EDPACS, Automation Training Center, 11250 Roger Bacon Drive, Suite 17, Reston, VA 22090.

Privacy Journal reports monthly on privacy issues as they relate to all levels of government and the private sector. Annual subscription: $65; 8 pages. Available from Privacy Journal, P.O. Box 8844, Washington, DC 20003.

Security Letter published twice monthly, focuses on industrial and commercial security, emphasizing corporate security planning, physical security systems, and personnel security. Annual subscription: $95; 8 pages. Available from Robert McCrie, Security Letter, 475 Fifth Avenue, New York, NY 10017.

Security Management is a monthly magazine intended for managers of security and loss prevention. Annual subscription: $16, or as part of an annual membership ($40) in the American Society for Industrial Security. A bimonthly newsletter is included in the membership. Available from Publication Department, ASIS, 2000 K St., N.W., Suite 651, Washington, DC 20006.

Security Systems Digest published every two weeks, provides news on the latest developments in security systems. It is written for commercial and industrial security specialists. Annual subscription: $62; 10 pages. Available from Washington Crime News Services, 7620 Little River Turnpike, Annandale, VA 22003.

Security World is a monthly magazine for industrial and commercial loss prevention specialists. Annual subscription: $15. Available from J. E. Thorsen, Security World, 2639 S. La Cienega Blvd., Los Angeles, CA 90034.

TDF Newsletter is a monthly newsletter on transborder data flow. It covers bills, laws, and decisions and reports on major meetings and activities relative to transborder data flow. Annnual subscription: $75. Available from Information Gatekeepers, 167 Corey Road, Suite 212, Brookline, MA 02146.

Transnational Data Report is a monthly international report on information policies and regulation. Annual subscription: $225. Available from Transnational Data Report, Postbox 6152, 1005 ED Amsterdam, Holland.

**National Bureau of Standards Computer
Security Publications**

Mailing addresses and telephone numbers for information for GPO and NTIS:

Superintendent of Documents
U.S. Government Printing Office
Washington, DC 20402
GPO Order Desk: (202) 783-3238

National Technical Information Service
5285 Port Royal Road
Springfield, VA 22161
Orders: (703) 487-4650
Information: (703) 487-4780

Prices change from time to time. Those listed below were accurate in late 1981.

Audit and Evaluation

Audit and Evaluation of Computer Security, edited by Zella Ruthberg and Robert McKenzie. NBS Spec. Pub. 500-19, October 1977. Reports on the recommendations of audit and computer experts to improve computer security audit procedures. Subjects covered included audit standards, administrative controls, program and data integrity, and audit tools and techniques. Order from GPO as SN 003-003-01848-1. $4.00.

Guidelines for Automatic Data Processing Risk Analysis. FIPS PUB 65, August 1979. Presents a technique for conducting a risk analysis of an ADP facility and related assets. Provides guidance on collecting, quantifying, and analyzing data related to the frequency of occurrence and the damage caused by adverse events. A specific example is given. Order from NTIS as NBS FIPS-PUB-65. $4.50.

Computer Crime

Criminal Justice Resource Manual on Computer Crime. A 438-page manual for investigators and prosecutors of computer crime, produced by SRI International. Order from GPO as SN 027-000-00870-4, 1979. $7.50.

Computer Crime. A 17-page brochure addressed to computer operations executives concerning computer crime, corporate policy, and reporting crimes to authorities. Order from the U.S. Department of Justice, Law Enforcement Assistance Administration, Washington, DC 20531.

Cryptography

A Key Notarization System for Computer Networks, by Miles E. Smid. NBS Spec. Pub. 500-54, October 1979. Describes a system for key notarization, which can be used with an encryption device to improve data security in computer networks. The key notarization system enables users to communicate securely via encrypted mail. It also protects personal files and provides a digital signature capability. Order from GPO as SN 033-033-02130-0. $1.75.

Computer Security and the Data Encryption Standard, edited by Dennis Branstad. NBS Spec. Pub. 500-27, February 1978. Includes papers and summaries of presentations made at a 1977 conference on computer security. Subject areas are physical security, risk assessment, software security, computer network security, applications, and implementation of the Data Encryption Standard. Order from GPO as SN 003-003-01891-1. $3.00.

Data Encryption Standard. FIPS PUB 46, January 1977. Specifies a mathematical algorithm to be implemented in electronic hardware devices and used for the cryptographic protection of computer data. Order from NTIS as NBS FIPS-PUB-46. $3.50.

Report of the Workshop on Cryptography in Support of Computer Security, by Dennis Branstad, Jason Gait, and Stuart Katzke. NBSIR 77-1291, September 1977. Reports on a workshop held at NBS to obtain expert opinions on the mathematical and statistical characteristics of the Data Encryption Standard. Summarizes the formal presentations and outlines the major issues raised. Order from NTIS as PB 27144. $5.25.

Report on the Workshop on Estimation of Significant Advances in Computer Technology, edited by Paul Meissner. NBSIR 76-1189, December 1976. Reports on a 1976 workshop held to solicit information on computer technology advances with potential impact on the security of the Data Encryption Standard. Presents the evaluations of computer industry, academic, and government experts on computer security design, architecture, and manufacturing.

Validating the Correctness of Hardware Implementations of the NBS Data Encryption Standard, by Jason Gait. NBS Spec. Pub. 500-20, November 1977. Describes the design and operation of the NBS testbed used for the validation of hardware implementations of the Data Encryption Standard (DES). This report provides the full specification of the DES algorithm, a complete listing of the DES test set and a detailed description of the interface to the testbed. Order from GPO as SN 003-003-01861-9. $1.60.

Data Base Security

A Data Base Management Approach to Privacy Act Compliance, by Elizabeth Fong. NBS Spec. Pub. 500-10, June 1977. Discusses how data base management systems can be used to implement Privacy Act requirements for the handling of personal data. Order from GPO as SN 003-003-01787-6. $1.40.

Data Base Directions: The Next Steps, edited by John Berg. NBS Spec. Pub. 451, September 1976. Proceedings of a workshop held in 1975 to develop information about data base technology for managers of data base systems. Covers five subject areas: auditing, evolving technology, government regulations, standards, and user experience. Order from GPO as SN 003-003-01662-4. $3.00.

General Computer Security

Accessing Individual Records from Personal Data Files Using Nonunique Identifiers, by Gwendolyn B. Moore, John L. Kuhns, Jeffrey L. Treffzs, and Christine

A. Montgomery. NBS Spec. Pub. 500-2, February 1977. Analyzes methodologies for retrieving personal information using nonunique identifiers such as name, address, etc. This study presents statistical data for judging the accuracy and efficiency of various methods. Order from GPO as SN 003-003-01726-4. $2.65.

Approaches to Privacy and Security in Computer Systems, edited by Clark Renninger. NBS Spec. Pub. 404, September 1974. Reports on a conference held at NBS to propose ways to meet government needs in safeguarding individual privacy and confidentiality of data. The views of legislators, citizens, computer industry associations and companies, professional societies, and public interest groups are presented. Order from GPO as SN 003-003-01319-6. $1.45.

Government Looks at Privacy and Security in Computer Systems, edited by Clark Renninger and Dennis Branstad. NBS Tech. Note 809, February 1974. Reports on a conference held at NBS to identify the legal, technological, and administrative needs and problems of government agencies in safeguarding individual privacy and protecting confidential data from loss or misuse. Order from NTIS as COM 74-50174. $4.50.

Controlled Accessibility Bibliography, by Susan K. Reed and Martha Gray. NBS Tech. Note 780, June 1973. A bibliography of 96 references to literature about computer security. Order from NTIS as COM 73-50533. $4.00.

Controlled Accessibility Workshop Report, by Susan K. Reed and Dennis Branstad. NBS Tech. Note 827, May 1974. Reports on technical meeting dealing with computer access controls, security audits, ADP management controls, personal identification, and security assessments. Order from NTIS as COM 74-50457. $5.00.

Glossary for Computer Systems Security. FIPS PUB 39, February 1976. Includes terms related to privacy and computer system security.

Guidelines for Automatic Data Processing Physical Security and Risk Management. FIPS PUB 31, June 1974. A handbook for structuring physical security and risk management programs for ADP facilities. Covers security analysis, natural disasters, failure of supporting utilities, system reliability, procedural measures and controls, protection of off-site facilities, contingency plans, security awareness, and security audit. Order from NTIS as NBS FIPS-PUB-31. $5.00.

Guidelines for Documentation of Computer Programs and Automated Data Systems. FIPS PUB 38, February 1976. Presents guidelines on the documentation needed at each stage of the software life cycle to provide for cost-effective operation, revision, and maintenance. Order from NTIS as NBS FIPS-PUB-38. $4.50.

Operating System Structures to Support Security and Reliable Software, by Theodore Linden. NBS Tech. Note 919, August 1976. Examines techniques to improve the design of computer systems. This study focuses on two system structuring concepts using modular software structures to satisfy security requirements and make systems more reliable. Order from GPO as SN-003-003-01658-6. $1.25.

Performance Assurance and Data Integrity Practices, by Robert L. Patrick, edited by Robert P. Blanc. NBS Spec. Pub. 500-24, January 1978. Details practices and methods that have been successful in preventing or reducing computer system failures caused by programming and data errors. The methods described cover large data processing applications, scientific computing applications, programming techniques, and systems design. Order from GPO as SN 003-003-01879-1. $2.20.

Security Analysis and Enhancements of Computer Operating Systems, edited by Theodore Linden. NBSIR 76-1041, April 1976. Examines types of security problems that arise in operating systems and suggests ways to improve security. Three commercial systems are analyzed and security flaws are classified. Order from NTIS as PB 257087. $4.50.

Network Security

Design Alternatives for Computer Network Security and *The Network Security Center: A System Level Approach to Computer Network Security*, by Gerald D. Cole and Frank Heinrich. NBS Spec. Pub. 500-21, January 1978. This two-volume study covers network security requirements and design and implementation requirements of a special computer dedicated to network security. It focuses on use of the Data Encryption Standard to protect network data and recommends procedures for generating, distributing, and protecting encryption keys. Order from GPO as SN 003-003-01881-3. $6.00.

Personal Identification and
Access Authorization

Evaluation of Techniques for Automated Personal Identification. FIPS PUB 48, April 1977. Discusses techniques for identifying individuals seeking access to computer systems. This report presents data for measuring the effectiveness of personal identification devices and for evaluating techniques and devices. Order from NTIS as NBS FIPS-PUB-48. $4.00.

The Use of Passwords for Controlled Access to Computer Resources, by Helen Wood. NBS Spec. Pub. 500-9, May 1977. Describes the need for and uses of passwords. Password schemes are categorized according to selection technique, lifetime, physical characteristics and information content. Order from GPO as SN 003-003-01770-l. $2.00.

Privacy

A Computer Model to Determine Low Cost Techniques to Comply with the Privacy Act of 1974, by Robert C. Goldstein and Henry H. Seward. NBSIR 76-985, February 1976. Presents a computer model to simulate costs of implementing the Privacy Act and to identify differences in cost that result from alternative approaches to implementing mandated safeguards. Order from NTIS as PB 250755. $4.50.

A Data Base Management Approach to Privacy Act Compliance, by Elizabeth Fong. NBS Spec. Pub. 500-10, June 1977. Discusses how data base management systems can be used to implement Privacy Act requirements for the handling of personal data. Order from GPO as SN 003-003-01787-6. $1.40.

A Methodology for Evaluating Alternative Technical and Information Manage-ment Approaches to Privacy Requirements, by Robert C. Goldstein, Henry H. Seward, and Richard L. Nolan. NBS Tech. Note 906, June 1976. Identifies the actions required of recordkeepers to comply with the Privacy Act and estimates the cost of these actions. Includes a computer model to aid in the selection of cost-effective safeguards. Order from GPO as SN 003-003-01630-6. $1.35.

Approaches to Privacy and Security in Computer Systems, edited by Clark Renninger. NBS Spec. Pub. 404, September 1974. Reports on a conference held at NBS to propose ways to meet government needs in safeguarding individ-ual privacy and confidentiality of data. The views of legislators, citizens, compu-ter industry associations and companies, professional societies, and public interest groups are presented. Order from GPO as SN 003-003-01319-6. $1.45.

Computer Security Guidelines for Implementing the Privacy Act of 1974. FIPS PUB 41, May 1975. Describes physical security, information management prac-tices, and computer system security controls that can be used by Federal ADP organizations to implement computer security safeguards. Order from NTIS as NBS FIPS-PUB-41. $3.50.

Computers, Health Records, and Citizen Rights, by Alan F. Westin. NBS Mono-graph 157, December 1976. Reports on the impact of computers on citizen rights in health recordkeeping. This study looks at the uses made of personal medical data and the trends in computerization of data. It recommends policy actions to guide the management of health data systems that respect citizen rights. Order from GPO as SN 003-003-01681-1. $4.55.

Computers, Personnel Administration, and Citizen Rights, by Alan F. Westin. NBS Spec. Publ. 500-50, July 1979. Reports on the impact of computers on citizen rights in personnel record keeping. This study traces the changing pat-terns of employment and personnel administration and examines the trends in computer use in personnel administration. It recommends policy actions to guide the management of personnel systems that respect citizen rights. Order from GPO as SN 003-003-02087-7. $8.00.

A Policy Analysis of Citizen Rights Issues in Health Data Systems, by Alan F. Westin and Florence Isbell. NBS Spec. Pub. 469, January 1977. A condensation of "Computers, Health Records, and Citizen Rights" (Monograph 157). Order from GPO as SN 003-003-01730-2. $1.05.

Exploring Privacy and Data Security Costs–A Summary of a Workshop, edited by John Berg. NBS Tech. Note 876, August 1975. Reports on workshop discus-sions about the cost of complying with the Privacy Act. Subjects covered include identifying costs, both direct and indirect, identifying benefits from implementing Privacy Act requirements, and allocating costs among those who receive benefits. Order from NTIS as COM 75-11113. $4.50.

Index of Automated System Design Requirements as Derived from the OMB Privacy Act Implementation Guidelines. NBSIR 75-909, October 1975. Lists requirements to be considered by administrative and technical personnel in com-plying with Privacy Act provisions relating to automated systems design and development. Order from NTIS as PB 246863. $3.50.

Security Controls and Safeguards

An Analysis of Computer Security Safeguards for Detecting and Preventing Intentional Computer Misuse, by Brian Ruder and J.D. Madden, edited by Robert P. Blanc. NBS Spec. Pub. 500-25, January 1978. Analyzes 88 computer safeguard techniques that could be applied to recorded actual computer misuse cases. Presents a model for use in classifying and evaluating safeguards as mechanisms for detecting and preventing misuse. Order from GPO as SN 003-003-01871-6. $2.50.

Considerations in the Selection of Security Measures for Automatic Data Processing Systems, by Michael J. Orceyre and Robert H. Cortney, Jr., edited by Gloria R. Bolosky. NBS Spec. Pub. 500-33, June 1978. Details methods and techniques for protecting data processed by computer and transmitted via telecommunications lines. This report identifies controls that can be instituted to protect ADP systems when risks and potential losses have been identified. Order from GPO as SN 003-003-01946-1. $1.40.

Computer Security Books and Articles

Burch, John G., Jr. and J. L. Sardinas, Jr. *Computer Control and Audit: A Total Systems Approach.* Wiley: 1978. Discusses the computer environment, a system of controls, and computer audit techniques. Each chapter has an excellent set of review questions, discussion questions, exercises, and problems. This material lends itself to a teaching/educational environment.

Canadian Institute of Chartered Accountants. *Computer Control Guidelines* and *Computer Audit Guidelines.* Toronto, 1970, 1975. An excellent early definition of controls and audit steps in computer systems.

Eason, T. S.; See M.E.; S.H.J. Russell; J.M. FitzGerald; and B. Ruder. *Systems Auditability and Control.* 3 vols. Altamonte Springs, Fla.: Institute of Internal Auditors, 1977. Presents the results of a $500,000 study performed by SRI International. Includes survey data on EDP audit departments and discusses audit tools and specific controls. The model used to represent the EDP environment and control areas of application systems can be very helpful.

FitzGerald, J.M. *Internal Controls for Computerized Systems.* Redwood City, Calif.: Jerry FitzGerald and Associates, 1978. Contains over 650 specific controls. A matrix structure is used to indicate the appropriate controls for a given resource and exposure in the different data processing component areas. The model used for the data processing function can be very helpful.

————.*Designing Controls into Computerized Systems.* Redwood City, Calif.: Jerry FitzGerald and Associates, 1981. Presents many controls for application systems and a methodology for designing controls into new systems or systems being modified.

Gibson, Cyrus F., and R.L. Nolan. "Managing the Four Stages of EDP Growth." *Harvard Business Review,* January-February, 1974, pp. 76-88. Presents a model of the stages of growth of EDP in organizations, including the point at which control becomes a major issue. It provides a framework for identifying and controlling the growth of EDP.

Hoffman, Lance J. "Computers and Privacy: A Survey." *Computing Surveys* (June 1969) vol. 1, no. 2, pp. 85-103. The "classic" survey on this subject.

Hsiao, David K.; D.S. Kerr; and S.E. Madnick. *Computer Security*. New York: Academic Press, 1979. Presents a review of research in computer security together with a critical assessment of the research.

International Business Machines. *Data Security and Data Processing*. 6 vols. White Plains, N.Y., IBM Data Processing Division, 1974. Presents the findings of the May 1972 data study project at MIT, TRW Systems, The State of Illinois, and IBM's Federal Systems Division and evaluates the IBM Resource Security System (RSS). Results of cost studies and implementation measurements as well as general papers on the subject are included in this unevenly presented but valuable collection.

Krauss, Leonard I. *SAFE: Security Audit and Field Evaluation for Computer Facilities and Information Systems*. East Brunswick, N.J.: Firebrand, Krauss, 1972. An extensive checklist audit guide for a complete review of security and controls in data processing facilities. Uses a weighted scoring that attempts to score quantitatively the merit of controls noted.

Krauss, Leonard I., and A. MacGahan. *Computer Fraud and Countermeasures*. Englewood Cliffs, N.J.: Prentice-Hall, 1979. A complete handbook on the software aspects of computer security.

Mair, William C., D.R. Wood, and K.W. Davis. *Computer Control and Audit*. Altamonte Springs, Fla.: Institute of Internal Auditors, 1978. The classic book on computer control techniques and auditing approaches. The authors are partners in the CPA firm of Touche Ross and Company. The Touche Ross Foundation (New York, N.Y.) has developed an excellent set of case study work problems—"Case Studies in Computer Control and Audit"—and keyed them to the book.

Martin, James. *Security, Accuracy, and Privacy in Computer Systems*. Englewood Cliffs, N.J.: Prentice-Hall, 1973. A most complete treatment on the subject of computer security.

Nolan, Richard L. "Managing the Computer Resource: A Stage Hypothesis." *Communications of the ACM*, July 1973, pp. 399-405. Presents the stage hypothesis as a description of the process of using the computer resource in an organization. Includes a stage of increased emphasis on control.

————."Managing the Crises in Data Processing." *Harvard Business Review*, March-April 1979, pp. 115-126. Expands analysis of the EDP environment based on the stages of growth of a company's DP function.

Parker, Donn B. *Crime by Computer*. New York: Scribner's, 1976. The definitive book on computer crime.

————.*Ethical Conflicts in Computer Science and Technology*. Arlington, Va.: AFIPS Press. The first book on ethics in the computer field. Contains forty-seven ethical scenarios and the opinions of thirty-five leaders in the computer field about each one.

————.*Computer Security Management*, Reston, Va.: Reston Publishing Company, 1981. A very good reference book covering a wide range of topics such as identification of assets and threats, risk assessment, computer abuse, and computer crime laws. It contains many ideas and techniques for defining and implementing a computer security program.

Patrick, Robert B., ed. *AFIPS System Review Manual on Security*. Montvale, N.J.: AFIPS Press, 1974. The results of a two-year study under the direction of a committee chaired by John Gosden of Equitable Life Insurance; it presents a set of guides for evaluation and a series of checklists to aid in the review of system security.

Saltzer, Jerome H. and Michael D. Schroeder. "The Protection of Information in Computer Systems," *Proceedings of the IEEE*. September 1975. A thorough discussion of the technical aspects of providing protection in computer systems. The most complete and most valuable discussion of the concepts of protection to date.

Westin, Alan F. *Privacy and Freedom*. New York: Atheneum, 1967. The earliest and one of the clearest books on the subject.

Index

ABOUT THE AUTHORS

Tom S. Eason

Tom S. Eason is manager of systems in the Controller's Division, Wells Fargo Bank, San Francisco. He has thirty-one years of experience in the information systems field as a technical professional, line manager, and consultant and has conducted seminars in EDP loss control in the United States and many foreign countries. For the last eight years he has been increasingly involved in EDP loss control, both as a consultant and as an author. Before his association with Wells Fargo, he was Assistant Director of the Information Systems Management Center of SRI International (formerly Stanford Research Institute) in Menlo Park, California, where he managed the EDP loss control consulting activities. During this time he also was a principal author of a basic book on EDP auditing, *Systems Auditability and Control*, published in 1977 by the Institute of Internal Auditors. Before joining SRI International, he held administrative and senior technical positions with Planning Research Corporation and in the aerospace industry. He is coauthor of a popular college text on data communications.

Douglas A. Webb

Douglas A. Webb is a senior management systems consultant in the Information Systems Management Center of SRI International in Menlo Park, California. He has had fifteen years of experience with information systems as a consultant, researcher, teacher, and programmer. For the last ten years he has focused on EDP security and loss control, performing consulting and applied research for commercial and government organizations. He has been project leader on more than twenty major consulting and research projects and has developed and presented numerous seminars on EDP loss control both in North America and overseas. After receiving a Ph.D. in computer sciences from Syracuse University, he became part of a team at Lawrence Livermore Laboratories conducting applied research in the security of operating systems. He has been supervising editor, author, and coauthor of numerous research reports and EDP auditing documents and is a Certified Information Systems Auditor.